MW01621180

Amazing Stories for Curious Minds

Written by Mateo Sommer

Illustrations by Henrique C. Rampazzo

Production management by Magdalene Ward

For information address LittleBigPage, 312 W. 2nd St #1934
Casper, WY 82601, United States.

Paperback ISBN: 9788367973786

First Edition

AMAZING STORIES for CURIOUS MINDS

MATEO SOMMER

You can **download the free audiobook** version of this book.

Go to the *last page* for more information!

CONTENTS

Prologue

In the heart of Washington, DC, stood the Smithsonian Institution—a place filled with treasures of every kind. There were dinosaurs and diamonds, spaceships and steam trains, robots and rockets, even giant fossils from long ago. It seemed impossible that so many wonders could be found in one place.

That afternoon, a yellow school bus pulled away from the National Mall. Inside, the children were still buzzing with excitement from the long day.

"I can't believe I saw a satellite!" one said eagerly.

"Big deal," another replied. "Did you see that giant gold nugget?"

"I thought the shark jaws were going to swallow me whole!" someone else added.

The bus filled with chatter and laughter until a firm voice called from the front. "Order!" Coach strode down the aisle, as serious as always, and at once the children quieted.

Their teacher rose and smiled warmly. "Thank you, Coach, but I think we can agree everyone did very well today. We discovered so many amazing things."

The principal, who had marched them quickly through the exhibits, gave a little nod from his seat. Around him, the children were already leaning against the windows, their eyelids heavy.

One by one, they drifted into dreams. Dreams just as wild as the wonders they had seen.

SCHOOL BUS
SCHOOL BUS

CHAPTER 1

The Race from Space

When Luna opened her eyes, all she could see was stars. They weren't like the stars in a cartoon when a character bumps their head. These were stars way up high, shining in the night sky. But if Luna's view through the window was real, that meant she was sitting in a spacecraft!

A familiar, frightened feeling filled Luna's body. It made her arms and legs wobble and her belly flip. Luna was afraid of a lot of things. She was terrified of the dark, the monsters beneath her bed, and next-door neighbor's barking dog. At school, she was scared to hold up her hand, even when she knew the answer. As Luna stared at the stars outside, her teeth began to chatter. Being in space was her biggest fear of all.

Luna turned away from the window and *screamed*. She was face to face with a spaceman! Behind his glass visor, the spaceman looked just as surprised.

Luna recognized his light blue eyes. She'd learned about this NASA astronaut on her trip to the museum. His capsule had blasted into space in 1962!

"You're John Glenn," Luna said. "You were the first American to circle the Earth."

The astronaut smiled. "I haven't completed an orbit *yet*. It looks like you've joined my mission, little one." He tapped the low ceiling above his head. "Welcome to *Friendship 7*!"

Luna looked around the cramped cabin. Every surface was covered with dials, blinking lights, and silver switches. The clutter reminded Luna of her dad's garage. She couldn't believe that *Friendship 7* had made it safely into space!

"We're traveling at seventeen thousand miles an hour," John said.

Luna gripped her seat. "That's faster than the freeway."

John didn't seem frightened by the speed. "We're passing over the night side of Earth," he explained. "That's the part facing away from the Sun." He pointed to the window. "Why don't you take a look?"

Luna took a deep breath. She leaned toward the window and peered through the glass. Far below, a giant globe glowed softly. Surrounded by the blackness of

space, Earth's oceans looked inky blue. In the distance, Luna saw city lights twinkling in the night. The beautiful sight took her breath away.

"Isn't that a swell view?" John asked.

Luna nodded, speechless. She felt dizzy, delighted and terrified by the height.

"We're over Western Australia now," John continued. "Look, the people in Perth have left their lights on for me. It's as pretty as a picture!"

John reached under his seat and pulled out a rectangular camera. It had a black case with a round lens, like something from an old movie. "Don't you love new technology?" he asked. "With this automatic camera, I can take photos of Earth."

But the astronaut's gloves had fat fingers. John tried to change the film in his camera, but he found it difficult. The film slipped away and floated right past Luna's face. She'd almost forgotten there was zero gravity in space!

Just then, Luna had a bright idea. "*I'll* take some pictures, if you like."

Luna pulled her cell phone from her pocket. She was only allowed to use it when she felt scared and wanted to call home, but she was sure her parents wouldn't mind, just this once. Opening the camera app, she took a few snaps through the window.

John stared at the cell phone in wonder. "This technology is from the future!" he declared. "Where on earth did you get it?"

Luna thought long and hard. "I think Mom got it at Target," she replied.

With each journey around the Earth, Luna grew a little less scared. John sat beside her, happily flicking switches. He seemed to be in complete control.

"This is mission control," a voice crackled over the radio. "Your three orbits are complete. It's time to return home."

KA-BOOM!

The capsule jolted suddenly, throwing Luna forward. All at once, her body trembled from head to toe.

"What's happening?" she screamed.

John wasn't shocked. "The retro rockets have fired," he replied calmly. "They're slowing the capsule down and changing its course."

Luna gripped the seat again. She hardly dared to ask her next question.

"Which way are we going now?"

She already knew the answer. *Friendship 7* was going down! When the capsule dropped, the cabin began to shake. Luna gripped her seat till her knuckles turned white.

But John didn't seem worried at all. "We're re-entering Earth's atmosphere," he explained. "Things may get a little warm."

The capsule shook from side to side, and the view outside got worse. Soon, orange flames were shooting past the window! The cramped cabin grew hotter every second as *Friendship 7* raced down from space. Crying in terror, Luna looked at John. To her astonishment, he wasn't even sweating.

"I don't get it!" she wailed. "Why aren't you scared?" She stared at her trembling hands. "How can I *ever* be as brave as you?"

John took hold of Luna's hand. It felt tiny inside his big glove!

"I have a secret to share with you," he said. "I've been scared all along. This is also *my* first time in space!" He smiled kindly at Luna. "Bravery is all about facing your fears. You can *only* be brave when you're feeling afraid."

A bright blue sky appeared outside the window and lit up the cabin. Luna breathed a sigh of relief. The race from space was almost over! When its parachute opened, the capsule slowed down with a jolt. Luna squeezed John's hand—but she *didn't* scream.

Friendship 7 floated down from the sky to the waves below. A few moments later, the capsule landed on the ocean with a gentle bump.

The landing shook Luna awake. Outside her window, traffic was crawling past. Luna couldn't see the ocean anymore, only her sleeping classmates. To her surprise, she was sitting on the school bus!

#1

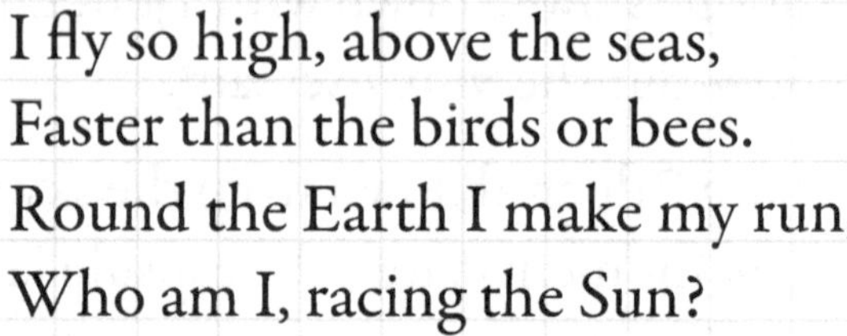

I fly so high, above the seas,
Faster than the birds or bees.
Round the Earth I make my run,
Who am I, racing the Sun?

#2

Which word doesn't belong with the others?

Rocket – Capsule
Spacesuit – Submarine

#3

1. John Glenn's spacecraft was called Friendship 7.
2. Astronauts in orbit travel about 17,000 miles per hour.
3. The first American to land on the Moon was John Glenn.

Which number is the twist (the false one)?

CHAPTER 2

Time to Fly

Sawyer brushed the sand from his eyes. He was standing on a gray beach that stretched into the distance. He couldn't see another person, nor any sign of the sky. As far as he could tell, it was completely covered in clouds! Looking up, Sawyer felt ashamed. He thought about a sentence on his recent report card. He could still hear his disappointed dad reading the words out loud.

"Sawyer's head is often in the clouds."

Sawyer wasn't sure if something was wrong with him. At school, he got lost in his daydreams for hours. When he wasn't staring out the window, he was great at writing stories. He often spent recesses reading with Theo. At lunchtimes, he made up amazing adventures with Ethan. But when Sawyer left his fantasy world, the real one seemed more difficult. Sometimes, he found it hard to do anything at all.

A ghostly *whirring* drifted across the beach. It sounded like a propeller! At that moment, Sawyer's body started to tingle. Suddenly, he *knew* that he'd come here to fly.

Black-and-white images flashed in his mind. Sawyer saw an old aircraft rolling along the sand. The biplane had a wooden frame and two fabric wings to keep it light. In 1903, the famous plane had made the first manned flight! Sawyer remembered the *Wright Flyer* from his visit to the museum. The two brothers who'd built it were called Orville and Wilbur.

Their plane hadn't been ready for takeoff right away. It had taken them *years* of hard work! The Wright brothers had learned from every crash landing, and one December day, they finally got it right.

Sawyer watched the plane rise into the air. The *Flyer* was flown by one of the brothers lying on his front. To Sawyer, it seemed like the shaky plane barely left the sand, but the cheering brother on the beach knew that he'd made history.

As the movie images faded, the beach was empty again. Sawyer prepared to fly by struggling to the top of a nearby dune. It didn't help that his legs were trembling. Nervously, he peered at the beach down below. He didn't want to fail and fall on his face! Closing his eyes, Sawyer took a deep breath. He bent his knees, jumped—and landed face-first in the sand.

Splat!

Sawyer brushed his eyes for a second time. "Ouch," he moaned. "I guess I hit the beach." As he wiped the sand away, he discovered he wasn't hurt. The crash landing hadn't been nearly as bad as he feared.

Sawyer decided to try again. When he climbed to his feet, he heard the ghostly propeller in the wind. He remembered that the *Flyer* had taken off from a rail in the sand, so instead of jumping from another dune, he began to run along the beach.

As Sawyer ran against the wind, it gusted in his face. It felt like a powerful force was trying to hold him in place! Sawyer pushed forward, but each step was harder than the last. Soon, the wind was howling around him. His head was filled with doubts.

"You're a disappointment," his dad's voice said.

"Your head is in the clouds," his teacher's voice added.

"You're going to fail," his own voice said. "You'll never do anything special."

Sawyer tried to ignore the doubts, but he couldn't block them out. He tripped, stumbled, and hit the be-ach again.

Splat!

This time, the landing hurt a little more. Sawyer lo-oked around, but no one had seen him fall. His cheeks were burning, but he wasn't sure why. He had no reason to be embarrassed!

After dusting himself off, Sawyer heard the propeller again. He thought about the Wright brothers, and that famous day on the beach. The first flight had only lasted for twelve seconds, but even that had taken many failed attempts.

Sawyer jumped to his feet. "You can *do* this," he told himself. "I believe in *you*."

He ran forward with confidence, spreading his arms wide like wings. As his doubts disappeared, his legs felt lighter. Before he knew it, his feet were leaving the gro-und. It felt like nothing was holding him down!

Flying was a fantastic feeling. Looping the loop, he whooped with joy. Sawyer soared through the air with the wind rushing through his hair.

"I love flying!" he declared. "It's just *plane* fun!"

Sawyer's feet touched down on the sand. He was tingling with excitement from head to toe! Although his flight had lasted less than a minute, it still felt very special. He had proved he could do anything, even if

it seemed difficult at first. Smiling proudly, he looked along the beach. Somehow, it felt like his whole world had changed.

To Sawyer's surprise, two men were waving at him. They were dressed in suits, so they weren't going swimming. One of the men had a big mustache that looked like the end of a brush. Sawyer recognized them right away. It was Orville and Wilbur Wright!

When he ran over to greet the brothers, they raised their bowler hats. "You did it!" Orville said. "I knew I wasn't wrong."

"He's right," Wilbur replied. "My brother said you wouldn't give up."

Sawyer blushed. "Have you been watching me?" he asked.

"Not only that," Wilbur replied, "we've been filming you too!'

He pointed to a strange box on legs with a handle attached to the side. Sawyer had never seen such an old-fashioned camera before.

"Congratulations!" Wilbur said. "You proved that nothing is impossible."

"He's right," Orville replied, "and we captured it all on camera."

The Wright brothers raised Sawyer onto their shoulders. Now, he didn't mind that his head was close to the clouds. "Here's to Sawyer," the brothers cheered together. "What he has done today will be an inspiration to everybody!"

#1

Two brothers built me with wood and pride.
I first left the sand with a shaky glide.
Twelve short seconds, yet history was made.
What am I, that humans first flew in and stayed?

#2

Which word doesn't belong with the others?

Propeller – Wing – Parachute – Engine

1. The Wright brothers tested their ideas first with kites and gliders.
2. The Wright Flyer's first flight was on December 17, 1903.
3. Charles Lindbergh helped the Wright brothers design their first plane.

Which number is the twist (the false one)?

CHAPTER 3

Attack of the Kraken!

HARPER WAS WOKEN suddenly from her nap. As she swung gently from side to side, a spray of salty water splashed her face! She was lying in a rope hammock, on board an old wooden boat. Looking out at the wide ocean, Harper smiled with excitement. Sailing the world was the kind of adventure she'd always dreamed about! Harper wished her parents could see the galleon's white sails. She longed to tell Ms. Miller about the size of the stormy waves. But even if she could, Harper wasn't sure the adults would believe her story. Although she was confident, grown-ups didn't always take her seriously.

Leaping from the hammock, Harper landed on her feet. Right away, she fell back on her bottom! The sloping deck was slippery with seawater. To make things worse, it was rocking back and forth. Harper stood up shakily. Finding her sea legs was harder than she thought.

A strong smell filled Harper's nose. *"Gross,"* she said, "something fishy is going on!"

Harper followed the powerful scent. She soon discovered five large nets filled with freshly caught fish. As the creatures flipped and flopped about, their scales dripped with water.

"Help!" yelled a fish, opening its mouth.

Jumping in surprise, Harper almost fell over again. When she heard the shout a second time, she realized she had been wrong—the sound was coming from the front of the boat!

At the prow of the ship, Harper saw a group of sailors. They wore loose blue shirts and red scarves around their necks. The terrified men were pointing at the water.

"Someone help!" a sailor yelled. "A cracker is coming to attack!"

Harper ran across the deck, trying not to slip. When the crewmen saw her approaching, they looked at each other in astonishment.

"What be a girl doing on board?" asked a sailor with a big beard.

"Might she be our new captain?" asked another. "The last one fell *overboard*!"

Harper frowned at the sailors. They were quite confusing. "Did you say a *cracker* was attacking?" she asked.

The sailors laughed. "Not a cracker," the man with the beard replied. "I be talking about a *kraken*. Of all the sea monsters I've met, the kraken be the scariest!"

The crewmen looked frightened again. When they turned back to the ocean, their faces went as white as the galleon's sails.

"I've never seen a sea monster," Harper said. "I'd better take a look for myself!"

Standing on tiptoe, Harper peered over the side of the ship. The sight of the rolling waves made her feel a little seasick. Beneath the surface, some kind of creature was rushing toward the boat. It burst out of the water, spraying Harper with another salty shower! The weird creature was pinky-red and longer than three people. It had eight arms covered with suckers, which stuck fast to the wooden boat. But the monster's two tentacles were the strangest of all—they were even longer than its body! Slithering out of the waves, the tentacles gripped the ship beside Harper's hands.

"Get back, lass!" a sailor shouted.

But Harper wasn't afraid of the creature. In the Natural History Museum, she had seen this *cephalopod* before. She knew that it lived in the deepest oceans, and it didn't like to be found. This incredible sea creature wasn't a monster at all!

The pale sailors huddled on the deck. They stared in terror at the two long tentacles.

"That is a giant squid," Harper explained. "Krakens don't exist."

The sailors looked suspicious. "You be just a girl," one man said. "What do you know about monsters?"

"Aye," another replied. "You must think we be fools."

Harper scowled. The sailors weren't taking her seriously.

"That is a giant squid," she repeated. "If you don't believe me, then you're all suckers!"

"Don't listen to the landlubber," the crewman with the beard said. "If we don't kill that kraken, we'll be dragged down to the depths."

The sailors followed their leader. He picked up a sharp spear with a long, wooden handle. Harper gasped. He was going to throw a harpoon!

"Stop!" she commanded. "I *am* your new captain. Don't kill that squid!"

One by one, the sailor's mouths dropped open,

but the bearded man didn't drop his harpoon. Thinking quickly, Harper tried to remember what she'd learned at the museum.

"If I *wasn't* a captain," she said, "I wouldn't know that giant squid don't hunt humans." She pointed at the tentacles clinging onto the galleon. "That creature isn't attacking us. It's hiding from something else."

Fwoom!

A huge plume of water shot out of the ocean. Harper was soaked by a third salty shower!

The crew was drenched too, and the bearded man dropped his harpoon in surprise.

Harper and the sailors splashed across the deck. On the other side of the ship, the squid was hidden from sight. Harper saw a massive whale coming up from the waves. She recognized the size of its huge, rectangular nose.

"That is a sperm whale," she declared, "the largest living predator with teeth. It's the only thing that will hunt a giant squid."

This time, the crew didn't argue. "What should we do?" the man with the beard asked.

Harper grinned. "I'm going fishing!"

She ran along the deck and grabbed hold of one of the full nets. Using all her strength, she dragged it back to the prow of the ship. The crewmen watched her in astonishment.

"Lift this net up!" Harper commanded, grabbing hold of the harpoon.

Gripping the sharp spear, she ripped the net open. The slippery fish slid out of it and tumbled into the water. "Have this fast food," Harper shouted, "and leave the squid alone!"

Showered by hundreds of fresh fish, the hungry sperm whale slurped them from the ocean. Once its huge belly was full, it sank out of sight. When she turned around, Harper couldn't see any tentacles either. Once it was safe, the giant squid had released its grip on the ship!

The galleon's crew jumped for joy. They were glad their new captain had saved them.

"Would you like some rum?" the bearded sailor asked. "We be having a celebration!"

Harper yawned and climbed into her hammock. "No thanks," she replied. "I'm a child." She laid down and closed her eyes. "And I never finished my nap."

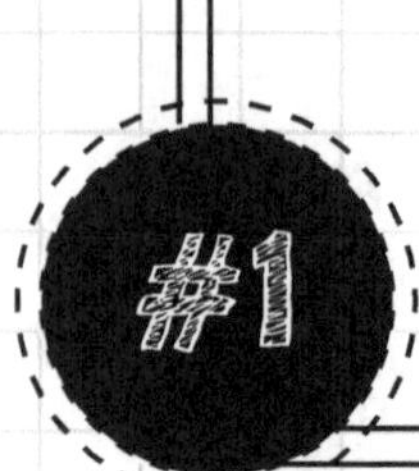

I live in oceans, deep and wide,
With tentacles, I try to hide.
A monster in a sailor's song,
But science shows they've got
it wrong. What am I?

#2

Which word doesn't belong with the others?

Kraken – Giant Squid
Octopus – Seahorse

1. The kraken was first described by scientists in 1980.
2. Giant squid have the largest eyes of any animal on Earth.
3. Sperm whales dive thousands of feet deep to hunt squid.

Which number is the twist (the false one)?

CHAPTER 4

The Bright Spark

In the Hall of Human origins, Adam felt all alone. The other fourth graders had rushed across the room to a model of a Neanderthal man. They pointed at his bumpy forehead and laughed at the shape of his long skull. Adam could have told his classmates a lot about prehistoric people. Shorter than modern humans, they were still strong, and their brains were just as big! But Adam's classmates never listened to him. Although he knew lots of facts, they always ignored his ideas. He wasn't surprised that the other students had left him behind.

Adam stopped by a glowing display called "The Birth of Fire." He peered at the replicas of early stone tools, which looked like the flint he took on camping trips. Most of all, Adam was drawn to a single, smoldering ember. Carefully cupped in two hands, the tiny flame looked like a precious object.

"What made fire *so* special?" he wondered. "I thought it was only used for cooking food."

Suddenly, the lights flickered out . . . and an icy wind blasted into his face! After forcing his eyes open, Adam couldn't believe what he saw. He was standing in a frozen forest, surrounded by towering pines and fir trees. As the trees' spiky branches trembled in the wind, Adam's skin broke out in goosebumps. His hoodie and jeans were no match for the bitter cold.

Adam whirled around in a circle. "Helloooo?" he shouted. "Is anyone there?"

The wind howled even louder, stealing his voice away. Shivering, Adam pulled his hood over his head. The museum was gone, along with his classmates. He really *was* all alone!

But to Adam's astonishment, someone had heard his cry. A group of eight wide-eyed children crept out from the trees. As they *crunched* toward him through the snow, Adam's jaw dropped open. The Neanderthal kids had nothing on their feet!

"I'm Adam," he greeted them, "and I'm a *Homo sapien*."

The puzzled children paused but didn't run away. Instead, the smallest ones pointed at his head.

"Of course!" Adam realized. "You must be wondering what happened to my ears." He pulled down his hood. "I'm wearing clothes, like you, but I *wish* I had one of your animal skins!"

An older child took a step closer. She was shorter than him, although her eyes seemed wise. Frowning at Adam, she pointed fearfully at the sky.

Bra-kooom!

A clap of thunder made everyone jump. Adam stared at the angry clouds above that grew darker by the moment. The wild-haired girl was warning him about an approaching storm.

"Let's go!" Adam said. "We need to get somewhere warm."

He followed the kids through the deep snow. Before long, his sneakers were soaked, and his feet were frozen. He expected that the barefoot children were heading to a cozy cave. But instead, they led him to a low shelter beneath a stony ledge that stuck out from the cliffside. As fat raindrops fell from the sky, Adam gulped. It was going to be a rocky night ahead!

The shuddering children crowded around a pile of sticks, looking at Adam with worried expressions. When a flash of lightning lit up the cliffside, their tearful eyes went even wider. For the first time, Adam noticed the splinters and scrapes all over their hands.

"You've been trying to make a fire," he realized, "but none of you know how to light it."

BRA-KOOOM!

As thunder boomed, Adam knelt on the ground. He was desperate to create a spark of hope for the children. Picking up two dry sticks, he rubbed them together to make heat. At the same time, he blew onto the pile, hoping to fuel a flame with oxygen. When his stick snapped, a child began to cry. Adam felt like doing the same.

But Adam didn't cry, and he didn't give up either. Instead, he whispered something that his grandpa had told him once on a camping trip. "Fire doesn't come easy. That's what makes it valuable."

Patting his pockets, Adam didn't find any flint, but he did pull out a long piece of string. Adam grinned. "*Now* we're cooking," he said. "Or at least, we will be soon."

Taking a curved piece of wood from the pile, Adam made a simple bow drill. Tying the string to both ends, he wound it around a straighter stick in the middle. When the drill moved back and forth, the spinning spindle created a lot of heat and friction. As the storm raged, the children huddled together, shielding Adam from the wind. They leaned in close, watching his drill with wonder.

Finally, Adam's hard work and patience paid off. With a bright spark, a soft glow, and a swirl of smoke, a precious flame flickered into life.

Adam was relieved to see the dancing flame. "Thank goodness I went to scout camp." But to his disappointment, the children didn't cheer. Instead, they gasped and ran away.

"Great," Adam moaned, protecting the flame. "I've been left on my own . . . *again*."

But the children hadn't really run away. Once more, they were helping him, by gathering fuel to build up the fire. Searching the shelter, they brought back bundles of dried moss and twigs. Before long, the fire was burning bright.

While Adam warmed his hands by the crackling flames, the Neanderthal children did the same. As their faces thawed, they grinned from ear to ear. Adam couldn't help smiling in return. Meanwhile, the older girl cooked for the group, roasting roots on the roaring fire. Although he wasn't the biggest fan of vegetables, Adam bravely took a bite.

"Not bad," he lied, "it tastes like potato—and just a bit like dirt."

The Neanderthal children couldn't understand Adam's words, but his feelings must have been clear on his screwed-up face. The children laughed and giggled with glee. Soon, even Adam was howling louder than the storm.

Tired out, the prehistoric kids fell asleep around the fire. As Adam listened to them murmur and snore, he felt an even greater warmth in his heart. Although they hadn't shared any words, the children had taught him something deeper than language. He'd learned that fire wasn't only for cooking. For the Neanderthals, it provided protection, connection, and survival.

Outside the shelter, the storm clouds rolled away. While stars shone in the midnight sky, the fire burned to embers. Watching their gentle glow, Adam's eyelids grew heavy. When he blinked, he was standing before the glowing display again.

Adam was back in the museum! He ran across the room. His classmates were still staring at the Neanderthal man.

"I can't believe we have a caveman project next week," Dylan complained. "I don't know *anything* about them."

“Well, they knew how to use fire,” Adam explained. “At first, it would have seemed impossible to create, but like all progress, it was made possible by people working together.”

For once, the other students didn’t run off. Maybe they sensed that his Neanderthal knowledge had somehow come from experience. To Adam’s surprise, they listened to him speak without dismissing his ideas. Now, all of them wanted to team up with him next week. As his classmates huddled around him, Adam smiled happily. This really was a dream come true!

I'm hard to tame yet bright to see.
I warm your hands and cook your tea.
I flicker, crackle, and chase the night—
What am I, glowing warm
and bright?

#1

Which word doesn't belong with the others?

#2

Embers – Sparks – Ash – Ice

1. Neanderthals lived during the Ice Age and used fire to keep warm and cook food.
2. A bow drill uses a cord to spin a wooden spindle on a fireboard until it makes a tiny coal called an ember.
3. The first matches were used in the Stone Age so cave families could light fires quickly.

#3

Which number is the twist (the false one)?

CHAPTER 5

Stella's Wild Ride

Stella yawned as she shuffled past the tractors, wagons, and engines. Everything in this part of the National Museum of American History smelled of polish and boredom. As her classmates walked ahead, a black car caught Stella's eye. It was parked behind some velvet ropes, as if it was a celebrity. Stella frowned at the old vehicle invented by Henry Ford. According to the plaque, his Model T Ford was "The car that changed America" in 1908! Stella rolled her eyes. She was sure her brothers would geek out about the vehicle. They loved to argue about engine power and pretend that girls knew nothing about cars.

Stella *was* interested in many mechanical things. She just preferred mending and solving problems over staring at the end result.

Sneaking under a rope, Stella crept closer to the car. It had silver headlamps and a simple windshield, and its roof was folded back. There was also a ledge along each side . . . with room for a person to stand.

Stepping onto the ledge, Stella leaned forward to feel the leather seats. "Big deal," she mumbled. "I still can't work out why this car is so special."

Vroom!

As the engine rumbled into life, the car lurched forward. Stella was thrown into the passenger seat. Before she knew it, the museum had vanished, and wind was whipping through her hair. To Stella's surprise, she was riding outside in the speeding automobile!

"Take these!" the driver shouted, passing her some goggles. "Don't get flies in your eyes."

Stella was too bewildered to reply. The man beside her was dressed in a three-piece suit. Gripping the wheel with leather gloves, he was wearing his own pair of goofy goggles. Through his lenses, he peered at Stella with confusion.

"I'm Buster!" he yelled over the roar of the engine. "You can't be a delivery driver. You're a *girl*!"

Stella's mouth dropped open. "My name is *Stella*. And being a girl doesn't mean—"

"No matter," Buster interrupted, "we can't turn back. We're already late!"

Shutting her mouth, Stella grimaced. She was sure she'd just swallowed a fly. "What are we late *for*?" she asked.

Buster grinned. "To make history! This is one of the first Model Ts. We're delivering it fresh from the factory in Detroit."

The automobile hit a bump, jolting Stella from side to side. Bouncing over a rock, it splash-landed in a puddle. Muddy water showered her.

Scowling, Stella brushed her overalls. "Can't we go another way?" she asked.

"*No* way," Buster replied with a chuckle, "this is the only road to Grand Rapids."

As the car lurched along the dirt road, Stella looked out at the flat fields. It looked like she was in the middle of nowhere. This wasn't modern Michigan where her grandparents lived! A horse-drawn wagon carrying bushels of corn clattered toward the Ford. When the horses heard the growling engine, they reared up in fear, and the angry wagon driver waved his fist.

"Oops," Stella said as they left the wagon behind. "I think we just invented road rage."

Buster steered the vehicle around several piles of manure. "At *last*, the road is clear," he declared. "It's time to reach top speed!" He yanked the throttle lever, slamming Stella against her seat. "Forty-five miles an hour!" Buster boasted. "*Nothing* can stop us now."

Bang!

Suddenly, the car shook. Stepping on the brakes, Buster swerved the car to a halt. To his horror, a tire had popped. Jumping out of the car, Stella noticed tiny nails in the dirt. Someone had scattered dozens of tacks, forcing the Ford to stop in its tracks.

"It's sabotage!" Buster exclaimed. "This vehicle is one of the first to be mass-produced. Mr. Ford makes cars that *anyone* can afford, but he's also made some enemies. Our competitors don't want us to deliver on time. Someone is trying to stop our historic journey!"

By the time Buster finished his speech, Stella had found a wrench in the trunk. "Do you want me to change the tire?" she asked. "You've got a spare on the back."

This time, Buster's mouth dropped open. "*You* know how to change a tire?"

"Of course," Stella replied, kneeling by the wheel. "My uncle showed me how. *He* doesn't mind that I'm a girl." She offered Buster the greasy wrench. "Unless you'd prefer to do it?"

Blushing, Buster stepped backward. "These *pneumatic* tires are new to me," he mumbled. "I haven't actually changed one yet."

Thanks to Stella's fixing skills, the spare tire was attached in minutes. But although the wheels were rolling again, the road ahead was still rocky. As the Ford approached the Thornapple River, Buster braked before a crooked wooden bridge. With twisted timbers and rotten boards, the wonky structure looked ready to fall apart. Now, Stella had *another* problem to solve. Could the heavy automobile cross the bridge before it collapsed?

"We should zoom over," Buster suggested, "the quicker the better!"

Stella shook her head. "We should drive as *slowly* as possible. If we spread out the car's weight, we won't overload the bridge."

Buster peered at Stella through his goggles. "Let me guess. You've built a bridge before?"

"No," Stella replied, "but I helped make my own bunk bed."

Gently, Buster pulled on the throttle, easing the vehicle forward.

Crack! Snap!

Beneath the wheels, the bridge's rotten boards began to splinter. Stella gripped the side of the car. Her heart was thumping hard!

"Don't make *any* sudden moves," she said, "or we'll never make it across!"

Slowly and steadily, the car crept over the bridge. The wood groaned and creaked under them. Luckily, Buster followed her advice, and to Stella's relief, they reached the other side.

At sunset, the Ford rolled into Grand Rapids. As its engine sputtered to a stop, the local folk cheered outside their new brick houses. Pulling off her goggles, Stella smiled and waved at the people. She was bruised from her journey, but she wasn't broken.

"Thanks for the ride, Buster," she said. "But in the future, you need some seat belts."

Buster wiped his brow. "I should be thanking *you*, Stella. One day, this world will run on wheels, and it won't matter *who's* holding the wrench, as long as they know how to use it!"

Facing the sunset, Stella closed her eyes for just a moment. When she opened them again, the street had disappeared. To her amazement, the famous Ford was parked back at the museum! There were no flies on the windshield anymore or muddy splatters on the side. But to Stella, the polished car still smelled of grease and excitement.

She scrambled out of the vehicle, hoping no one had noticed, but as she ducked under the velvet rope, Dylan walked around the corner. "Have you been sitting in that Ford?" He snorted. "Cars are such a *boy* thing."

Stella smirked. "There's no such thing," she said. "Only bridges you haven't crossed yet."

Built to make the country strong.
From muddy tracks to towns I see—
Which early car helped set us free?

#1

#2

Which word doesn't belong with the others?

Hand crank – Magneto
Carburetor – Fuel injector

1. Henry Ford's assembly line helped build cars faster and made them affordable for many families.
2. Seat belts were standard safety equipment in the very first Model T cars.
3. The Model T Ford could reach a top speed of about 45 miles per hour.

#3

Which number is the twist (the false one)?

CHAPTER 6

Tunes in the Tomb

Aria blinked in the darkness. Her eyes were still getting used to the spooky passage. She seemed to be underground, and the sloping tunnel went even deeper. A cobweb brushed against Aria's hair, making her shiver. She tried her best to forget that she was on her own! At school, she had plenty of friends, although she never picked the games they played. Sometimes, Madison got to choose. When Harper was playing, she led the way. But Aria didn't mind, as long as everyone was happy. Right now, though, she couldn't see any sign of her friends. Stuck in this dark, narrow tunnel, she was lost and all alone.

Oooooooh...

A terrible wail echoed along the passage. Aria's body was covered with goosebumps! Whoever had made the sound, they weren't far away. Peeking her head around the corner, Aria *screamed* with fright. She'd almost bumped into a dusty mummy!

History was one of Aria's favorite subjects. She'd read a great deal about the Ancient Egyptians, but Aria was sure that *all* her classmates would recognize a mummy. The bandages wrapped around this woman's body were a big giveaway.

"Hello," the mummy said, "my name is Tentkhonsu."

"Achoo!" Aria replied, sneezing from the dust.

"Tentkhonsu," the mummy repeated, correcting Aria. "You can call me *Su* for short. I come from the city of Thebes," she explained. "Have you been there before?"

The ancient city wasn't there anymore, but Aria decided not to upset Su by telling her.

The tunnel led to a wide chamber with a high ceiling hidden by shadows. The bandaged lady led Aria across the room. Her feet were tied together, so she tiptoed very slowly.

"Please forgive all the dust," Su said. "It seems my cleaner hasn't been here for a while." She pointed to the middle of the chamber. "Do you like my bed? It's really rather beautiful."

When Aria saw the mummy's bed, she recognized it right away. It was a wooden coffin! She'd seen one on

display when her class visited the museum. The mummy's coffin had a picture carved on its lid. It looked like a woman whose arms were crossed. She had a long headdress, and her whole body was painted with colorful *hieroglyphs*.

"My people used pictures and symbols," Su said, "instead of writing words."

"I know," Aria replied. "These are instructions for bringing you back to life."

Aria covered her mouth. Did the mummy know that her bedroom was really a tomb?

Su laughed. "Don't be so silly. I only took a nap."

"In that case," Aria replied, "you overslept by three thousand years."

Oooooooh...

When Su wailed, Aria felt bad. She only wanted to share what she knew about mummies. She didn't mean to upset her! "I'm so sorry," she said. "How can I make you happier?"

But to Aria's surprise, the mummy wasn't sad. She was only doing some vocal exercises! Su blew a raspberry, sang a few scales, and then she wailed some more.

"I'm a singer," she said, when her warmup was finished. "I used to perform at festivals."

"Wow," Aria replied, "I wouldn't have guessed."

"My voice has gone all croaky," Su said. "That's what you get from too much *coffin*."

Suddenly, the mummy did sound sad. She tiptoed around the empty tomb, staring into the shadows. The singer seemed to be dreaming of her ancient life! Aria wished she could help somehow but couldn't think of a bright idea. Just like Su, she was totally in the dark, and the dusty tomb was deathly quiet.

Aria looked at the wooden coffin. She ran her hand along the rows of hieroglyphs. The symbols explained how to restore life in the underworld. What if Su could do just that?

"We should put on a concert," Aria said. "You can be the star performer!"

Su turned around. "I'd be the *only* performer," she said sadly.

"That doesn't matter," Aria replied. "What matters is that singing makes you happy!"

The mummy smiled. It seemed she liked Aria's idea. "You'll be the only person in the audience," Su said.

Aria smiled. "I'll clap loudly!"

Su took to the stage. Climbing on top of the coffin lid, she performed her biggest ancient Egyptian hits. Listening to Su sing, Aria got goosebumps again. Now that the croak was gone from her throat, the mummy had a beautiful voice!

As the tunes echoed around the tomb, Aria jumped to her feet. "I can hear the beat in my head," she declared. "It's impossible *not* to dance!"

Aria jived and jumped and wiggled. She danced till her feet were sore. On stage, Su grinned and twirled around. She was having the time of her afterlife!

At the same time, the beat grew louder. It sounded like someone was marching their way. A long line of excited mummies hurried into the room. Crowding around the coffin, they screamed for Su. The singer had awakened her biggest fans! Before long, the tomb was full of dancing mummies.

After a while, Su's bandages started coming loose. "This is my last song," she announced. "It's time to wrap up the concert."

When the show was over, the tired mummies shuffled back to their tombs. As for Aria, she was almost dead on her feet, so she sat to rub her feet. While doing so, she listened to Su wail softly to soothe her voice.

"You were awesome," Aria said. "You brought life back to the underworld."

"It was *your* idea," Su replied. "Thanks to you, everyone is happy."

Su climbed into her coffin and wished Aria goodnight.

"I hope you have a nice, long sleep," Aria said.

As she left the tomb, Aria felt proud of herself. With no one else to lead the way, she'd taken charge of her own adventure. She climbed up the sloping tunnel without feeling lonely. Now, there was nothing scary about the darkness.

I'm wrapped in cloth from head to toe.
I lived long ago, that much you know.
I sang at feasts where crowds would cheer.
Who am I that's standing here?

#1

Which word doesn't belong with the others?

#2

Coffin – Bandages
Hieroglyphs – Telescope

1. Ancient Egyptians built the pyramids as tombs for their pharaohs.
2. Su the mummy was buried in the city of Rome.
3. Hieroglyphs were made of pictures and symbols.

#3

Which number is the twist (the false one)?

CHAPTER 7

Mission: Missing Money!

Ethan could hardly keep his eyes open. As he stood before the bank vault, he was still half asleep. The round door was attached to the wall with huge hinges and silver screws. Ethan noticed the locks and bolts that normally kept it closed. The giant door looked just like one he'd seen at the museum. The door there guarded a gallery full of old coins and paper money.

Ethan wondered why the vault in front of him was open. He also wondered why he was wearing pajamas!

"Sorry to drag you out of bed," a familiar voice said, "but we have a serious problem."

Ethan's eyes widened. The man marching toward him was Coach Lopez! Weirdly, the sports teacher was wearing a suit. The two men behind him were both wearing shades. Ethan had no doubt he was in big trouble. For some reason, it was always Coach who caught him hiding by the lockers at school. In Ethan's imagination, the world was one big spy movie. He loved to creep along the hallways carrying a walkie-talkie. Sometimes, Ethan's friend Sawyer joined in the action. The two of them created the most incredible stories! It was always Coach who ended the game, and every time, he told Ethan to take school more seriously.

Ethan gulped. "What's the problem, Coach Lopez?"

"You mean *Agent* Lopez," the frowning man replied. "I'm here to give you an important mission. A $100,000 bill has been stolen from this vault. The CSS needs *you* to get it back."

"Who's the CSS?" Ethan asked. "Coach and the Silly Shades?"

Agent Lopez sighed. "The Child Spy Services," he replied. "Please take this seriously."

Ethan rubbed the sleep from his eyes. Discovering he was a spy was a big surprise! Ethan gave the bill some serious thought. He remembered reading about it at the museum. It had been printed in 1934, with a picture of President Woodrow Wilson on the front. The $100,000 bill was never used by the public. It was given to federal banks instead, to pay for large amounts of gold.

"I don't get it," Ethan said. "How is a single piece of paper worth *that* much money?"

"Money can be any object," Agent Lopez replied, "if everyone agrees on its value. Humans have always traded pieces of metal, but they've also swapped seashells, salt bars, and stones.

That's why a paper bill can be as valuable as gold."

Ethan was still feeling tired. "This mission," he said, "can I choose *not* to accept it?"

"No," Agent Lopez replied, spinning him around on the spot.

Suddenly, the agents were marching Ethan away!

Outside, a shiny black car was parked under a stre-etlamp. Climbing in the back, Ethan found a pile of clothes on the seat. There was a pinstriped suit, some grown-up shoes, and a hat with a wide brim. He thought it might be a fedora.

Ethan wriggled into the clothes. "Wait a minute," he said, "why do *I* have to get the stolen bill back?" He pointed at the two other agents. "Why don't you send these men in black?"

Agent Lopez was sitting in the driver's seat. As he steered the car through the dark city streets, he looked at Ethan in the rearview mirror. "You *could* be my best agent," he explained, "but first, you must learn to stop fooling around. Think of this as a training mission."

Ethan scowled and folded his arms. "So, you're sending me into the lion's den?"

"No," Agent Lopez replied. "You're going to the gangsters' hideout."

The car pulled up silently to the sidewalk. On the other side of the street, Ethan saw a single-story warehouse. The crooked wooden building looked battered and abandoned. Ethan trembled as he crept toward the warehouse, but it wasn't the cold night wind that made him shiver. On the sloping roof, a child-sized window was glowing softly. Since the skylight was shining, someone *had* to be inside.

Pulling down the brim of his hat, Ethan pushed open the front door. When he saw the grizzled gangsters inside, he almost ran away! The scar-faced men were sitting on a ring of broken barrels. At the center of the circle, on another barrel, was the $100,000 bill!

Hearing footsteps, the men stopped whispering. They turned toward the door and glared at him. "Hold it, buster!" a gangster with whiskers said. "This is a private meeting. Whaddya think you're doin' here?"

"Sorry for busting in," Ethan replied, "but *I'm* a gangster too. The name's Shorty McGee!"

To Ethan's relief, the men believed his disguise.

He took his place in the gangsters' circle, feeling pleased with himself. His mission was right on target! The men began to whisper again. It seemed the gangsters were working out how to spend the stolen note.

"We should buy a million cola bottles," said a gangster with smooth cheeks.

"Sugar is bad for you, Babyface," mumbled a gangster with no teeth.

"Let's bribe the President," another suggested, "to put all the kids in jail. The cells would be full of little punks, and there wouldn't be any room for criminals!"

All the gangsters laughed, and Ethan joined in. He didn't want to seem suspicious. But at that moment, a gust of wind blew through the open doorway. When his fedora flew off, Ethan gulped. His cover as a gangster was blown!

"I *knew* it," the man with whiskers snarled. "No one has a name like Shorty McGee."

"You're right," another man replied. "That's why you're our leader, Shifty Macnee!"

As the scary crooks closed in, Ethan looked around in panic. In his stiff, grown-up shoes, he couldn't run away from the gangsters. He *had* to think on his feet! Suddenly, he saw the child-sized window above his head.

Snatching the stolen bill, he leaped onto a barrel. As the angry gangsters grabbed at his heels, Ethan escaped through the skylight window!

Outside, Ethan dove into the back seat of the car. As Agent Lopez drove away, the tires made an ear-splitting *shriek*.

"I got the bill!" Ethan said, feeling incredibly tired.

"You *fit* the bill," Agent Lopez replied. "You proved you're my best agent."

Ethan tried to keep his eyes open. He didn't want to miss this unusual praise! "Does that mean I took my mission *seriously*?" he asked.

Agent Lopez frowned. "Forget about being serious," he replied. "It was your *imagination* that made you think quickly. No one else could have fit through that window!" He smiled at Ethan in the rearview mirror. "Are you ready for your next mission, young man?"

"No thanks," Ethan replied, letting his eyelids close. "I'm way too sleepy."

#1

I jingle. I fold. I help you buy.
From sweets to shoes, I'm the reason why.
I come as paper, metal too—
What am I that's used by you?

#2

Which word doesn't belong with the others?

Seashell – Salt bar
Gold coin – Credit card

#3

1. The $100,000 bill was only used for transfers between banks.
2. Woodrow Wilson, the 28th US President, is pictured on the bill.
3. The $100,000 bill is still printed today and can be found in wallets.

Which number is the twist (the false one)?

CHAPTER 8

A Brush with Fame

THEO STARED at the man in the painting. His wavy orange hair was streaked with green, and his pale skin was a mix of blue and yellow. The colors barely made sense at all! That was one of the reasons Theo loved art. Even if the colors *seemed* wrong, they still looked right on the canvas.

The painting was a famous self-portrait of Vincent van Gogh. The artist had painted himself in front of a mirror, holding his palette of colors, but the beautiful picture didn't make Theo happy. The painter's blue eyes were full of sorrow. What had made Vincent van Gogh so sad?

Theo wished his friend Sophia was here to see the portrait. At school, the two of them painted quietly together. Theo wasn't shy, but he wasn't as loud as Ethan. He liked to think *before* he started speaking, and he didn't like it when Eli teased him for taking too long.

Theo was the only kid in the gallery. He'd come here with Ms. Miller. She knew how much he loved painting, so she'd taken him to the National Gallery of Art, next door to the museums. Looking around, Theo realized that Ms. Miller was missing. Surely, she wouldn't have left him on his own. Feeling nervous, Theo decided to stay where he was. That way, his teacher would be able to find him again.

Theo turned back to the self-portrait. On the canvas, Vincent was surrounded by blue brushstrokes. They looked like sad thoughts spinning around his head. Leaning closer to study the strokes, Theo lost his balance. Before he knew it, he was falling into the frame.

Thwump!

Theo's backside landed on a hard, wooden floor. He looked in amazement at the brightly painted room. The walls were sky blue, the window frame was green, and a red blanket was spread across the yellow bed. On a nearby table, Theo saw a beautiful vase of sunflowers, but there wasn't much time to admire the room. Suddenly, an artist's easel fell onto the floor beside him. A second later, the canvas followed.

Thwump! Thwump!

Scrambling to his feet, Theo's cheeks turned bright red. Vincent van Gogh was right behind him!

Standing beside a tall mirror, the painter frowned at the fallen canvas.

"I'm *so* sorry," Theo said. "I didn't mean to drop in like that." He picked up the easel and the unfinished portrait. "I hope your work isn't damaged."

Theo stepped away from the flame-haired man. He was worried the famous artist might have a fiery temper! But to his surprise, Vincent simply sighed.

"Don't worry," he said sadly. "The painting is awful anyway."

Theo didn't agree, but he stayed silent. That was often the best thing to do when someone was upset. If you gave them time to talk, they might explain their feelings. But Vincent didn't say another word. Putting down his brush and paint palette, he turned and left the room.

Theo hurried after him, clomping down the wooden stairs. Stepping outside the yellow house, he squinted in the bright sunlight. Out here in the country, the world was filled with color! High above, the blue sky was brighter than the bedroom. The trees were the deepest green that Theo had ever seen, but the wide, golden fields were the most beautiful of all. The tall wheat stalks waved at the farmers, reminding them about the harvest.

Theo felt warm and content. He was standing in a painting that had burst into life!

Unlike Theo, Vincent hadn't stopped to admire the view. He was already plowing his way through the fields! Theo watched as he vanished into a wall of wheat.

"Wait!" he yelled. "Come back!"

Theo gave chase through the waving stalks. As he followed in Vincent's footsteps, he remembered some facts he'd learned about the artist. The Dutch painter had moved from Paris to the French town of Arles in 1888. But although Vincent's work grew brighter in the country, his dark mood didn't improve. The artist had been *so* unhappy, he'd even tried to cut off his ear. Theo hoped that Vincent would talk to him. If he did, he'd do his best to listen.

Finally, the painter stopped running. Theo caught up with him at the far side of the field. Vincent was staring at the bright blue sky while tears streamed down his face.

"I know what you'll ask me," he cried. "How can I be sad in such a beautiful place?"

Theo paused to catch his breath. It gave him a chance to think about his reply. "I don't think it's strange you're upset," he said, "but *if* you'd like to, you can tell me why."

Theo could only hear the wind whistling through the wheat. He wasn't sure if Vincent van Gogh was going to speak, but to his surprise, the artist sat down. Theo crouched beside him on the golden ground.

"My pictures aren't good enough," Vincent said, "and nobody likes them. My biggest fan is my brother, and he's always lending me money." He sighed and wiped tears from his face. "How can I call myself a painter when I've only sold one picture?"

Finally, Theo understood the reason for Vincent's sadness. The artist thought he was a failure because he hadn't made any money from his work. Theo knew he couldn't make Vincent rich, but perhaps he could give him an even greater gift.

"Your paintings are *beautiful*," Theo said. "One day, in the future, crowds of people will rush to see them in galleries."

"In the *future*?" Vincent mumbled. "That's no good to me now."

"Do you want to know *why* people love your paintings?" Theo asked.

"I guess so," the artist replied grumpily.

Theo smiled. "People love how your paintings make them feel. When I stare at your *Starry Night*, the world is a magical place. When I look at your *Self Portrait*, I share all your sadness. And every time I see your *Sunflowers*, my heart is filled with joy." He jumped to his feet and held out his hand. "So, don't you think you should finish your work?"

Vincent didn't reply. Instead, he grabbed Theo's hand.

Theo and Vincent returned to the yellow house. Back in the bedroom, the famous artist picked up his paintbrush again.

"Thank you, Theo," Vincent said. "You've given me a new reason to paint. Your thoughtfulness makes you very special. Don't let *anyone* tell you otherwise."

Thwump!

When Theo jumped through Vincent's mirror, he landed back in the gallery. Somewhere around the corner, Ms. Miller was calling his name. Taking a final look at the portrait, Theo smiled with delight. The man in the picture looked happy at last. Vincent van Gogh was smiling!

#1

I swirl the sky with yellow and blue.
I paint my feelings, old and new.
Though life was hard, my art shines bright.
Who am I who painted Starry Night?

#2

Which word doesn't belong with the others?

Palette – Easel – Paintbrush – Violin

#3

1. Vincent van Gogh moved to the French town of Arles in 1888.
2. Vincent van Gogh became rich and famous while he was alive.
3. Vincent van Gogh painted over 2,000 artworks in his lifetime.

Which number is the twist (the false one)?

CHAPTER 9

A Mississippi Myth

Madison screwed up her eyes. The wide river was dazzlingly bright! Up ahead, the main branch of the river curved to the left, while a smaller river branched off to the right. Madison guessed she was sailing up the Mississippi. Where else would she be on board a steamboat?

When she heard a whistle, Madison whirled around. She was standing at the bow of the boat in the shadow of two tall chimneys. There was a big, wooden wheel at the stern of the ship. As its paddles pushed through the water, the boat moved forward. Madison had seen a steamer before, but that had only been a model in the museum. This ship was six times longer than her classroom!

On top of the pilot's cabin, a silver whistle *tooted*. It looked like the boat was approaching a port! The steamer's crew hurried into view. They were dressed in overalls and dirty caps, and they all had mustaches. Although their faces were streaked with soot, the men seemed cheerful. As they rolled heavy sacks across the deck, they whistled a happy tune.

"Excuse me," Madison said. "Where are we sailing?"

The astonished crewmen stopped whistling. It was like they'd never seen a child before! "Are you traveling on your *own*?" a man with a crooked nose asked. "I don't understand modern kids."

"We're so old," a wrinkled man added. "I can't believe it's 1906!" The other men laughed loudly, displaying their missing teeth.

"We're sailing to Vicksburg," a man with bushy eyebrows explained. "That's where this cargo of grain is going."

When the crewmen heard the name of the city, they suddenly went quiet. Silently, they watched as the steamboat turned to the right. The men's pale faces made Madison nervous.

"What's so scary in Vicksburg?" she asked.

The wrinkled crewman leaned close. Madison could see hairs sprouting from his ears. "There's a myth about a local witch," he whispered, "who turns sailors into catfish.

Even the mighty Mississippi is afraid of the witch. Thirty years ago, the river turned left to avoid her."

"But the city of Vicksburg was left without a port," the crooked-nosed crewman explained, "so the people there changed the course of the smaller Yazoo River. Now, it flows past the city and into the Mississippi, and steamers can stop at Vicksburg again."

When the steamboat docked at the smoky port, there were horses and carts waiting for the cargo. Sweating, the crew heaved the heavy sacks overboard. They were eager to sail home as soon as possible.

As the crewmen unloaded the grain onto the dockside, a sobbing woman approached the boat. Her shawl was raggedy, and her hair was untidy. Although she was crying, she had a kind face. Seeing Madison, the old lady fell onto her knees. "Please help me," she begged. "My sister is ill! She lives downriver in Natchez, but I can't afford the stagecoach fare."

"I'm sorry to hear that," Madison replied. "Of course you can travel with us."

"Thank you," the grateful woman said, shuffling up a wooden ramp.

But as the steamer set sail from Vicksburg, not everyone welcomed Madison's guest. When the crewmen saw the woman on board, they all began to protest!

"Her hair is a mess," the man with bushy eyebrows sneered.

"Her clothes are rags," the man with a crooked nose replied.

"She might be a witch," the man with wrinkles mumbled. "After all, she's old and ugly."

Madison frowned. The men were wrong, but if she argued with them, they might be mean to her too! At school, Madison liked to be liked. She always avoided getting into fights. When Harper picked a game to play, Madison never disagreed. Even when Theo was teased, she kept her mouth shut. As the grumbling crewmen walked away, Madison felt relieved. Although they were very rude, she didn't want to rock the boat.

The steamer sailed down the Mississippi, which sparkled in the sun. Sitting at the bow of the ship, Madison felt miserable. The crewmen wouldn't share any of their food with the old lady, and since Madison was now her friend, they refused to feed her too. When the woman started crying again, Madison felt like doing the same.

"Don't worry," Madison said, "it's smooth sailing from here. You'll see your sister soon."

Suddenly, the steamboat jolted to one side. The motion almost threw Madison overboard!

Panicking, the crewmen hurried to the bow. They were even paler than before.

"Oh no!" the wrinkled man wailed. "We must have hit a snag!"

Madison knew that snags were bad news. In shallow parts of the Mississippi, there were fallen trees and branches beneath the water. When steamers hit them, they often sank! Madison watched the crewmen lower long, wooden poles. Poking them into the river, they tried to free the ship. Hearing a terrified scream, Madison turned around. To her horror, the old woman had fallen into the water.

"Help!" she yelled. "I can't swim!"

Madison ran over to the crew. "Come quickly," she said. "I think she's going to drown!"

But the men with mustaches shook their heads. They refused to rescue the helpless lady!

"That river is full of alligators," the bushy-browed man warned. "If you go swimming, they'll snap you up."

As the crew laughed, Madison felt mad. Now, she didn't care if the men liked her or not. "You're selfish," she said sternly. "I wish I'd told you sooner! You've treated that woman *awfully*. I'm going to save her myself!"

Madison balanced on the edge of the boat. She was frightened, but she tried to forget about the alligators. When she dove into the water, it was shockingly cold! Grabbing the woman under her arms, Madison helped her climb back on board.

"I'm so grateful," the old lady said. "Thank you for your kindness again."

For a moment, Madison lay on the deck. She was freezing cold and dripping wet. But thankfully, she didn't shiver for long. When the old lady waved her hand, Madison's clothes dried in an instant!

Madison stared at the woman in astonishment. "You've got magical powers!" she said. "Does that mean you really *are* a witch?"

A smile crossed the lady's lips. "Yes," she replied, "I *am* a witch. With the power to do both good and bad." She waved a finger across the deck. "The magic I choose all depends on how I'm treated by others."

Whirling around, Madison *gasped*. The steamboat's crew had vanished. Instead of the men, there were three catfish with mustaches, flipping and flopping around on the deck!

#1

I puff out smoke and make a loud sound.
I carry grain and goods around.
I turn my wheel through waters wide.
What am I, with paddles at my side?

#2

Which word doesn't belong with the others?

Steamboat – Paddlewheel
Chimney – Stagecoach

1. The people of Vicksburg built a brand-new river to replace the Mississippi when it moved away.
2. The Mississippi River is one of the longest rivers in the United States.
3. In 1906, steamboats were a common way to transport cargo along the river.

#3

Which number is the twist (the false one)?

CHAPTER 10

The Crying Dinosaur

LEVI HAD BEEN splashing through the swamp for ages. The air was sticky, and the squishy ground had already soaked his sneakers, but Levi had a much bigger problem. Where in the *world* was he going? Wading beneath some flowering fruit trees, Levi froze. Someone nearby was crying.

Levi followed the sad sound through the swamp. It led him to a sandy bank shaded by palm trees. When Levi arrived, he couldn't believe his eyes. He'd discovered a crying dinosaur!

The duck-billed reptile was the size of a truck. It had big back legs and a thick, flat tail.

Although it looked powerful, Levi knew why the creature was so upset. He'd seen a similar skeleton at the museum, in the famous Hall of Fossils. The *Edmontosaurus* on display there was labeled "The Last Dinosaur."

Levi crept closer to the crying creature. "I'm sorry," he said. "You must be so lonely."

A tear rolled down the dinosaur's beak. "I'm not *lonely*," he replied. "I'm being bullied, and I don't want anyone to know."

It seemed that *this* creature wasn't the last of his kind. Somehow, Levi felt even worse for the dinosaur. He had also been teased by bullies in the past. It was only thanks to his friend, Aaron, that Levi had learned to stick up for himself. But this was the Late Cretaceous Period, sixty-six million years ago. Aaron wasn't around, so Levi would have to be this dinosaur's best buddy.

"You don't need to feel ashamed," he said, "and it's important you tell a grown up."

The *Edmontosaurus* stopped sobbing. "Thank you," he replied, "but I ran away from my family. To reach the herd, I'll need to trek across the mountains."

Levi smiled. "Then I'll come with you."

The rocky hills were not quite mountains yet. Levi wondered how much higher they would rise in the future. Maybe he was exploring Cretaceous Colorado! He followed his dinosaur friend, climbing the hillside in big strides. It was tough work keeping up with him.

"Slow down," puffed Levi. "I'm small, and I only have two legs!"

"Sorry," replied the *Edmontosaurus*. "I've never met anyone who didn't walk on all fours."

As Levi scrambled up the stony slope, the pine needles crunched beneath his sneakers. Soon, he heard another sound. A growling dinosaur was blocking the path!

The *Edmontosaurus* stopped dead in his tracks. "Don't get any closer," he whispered.

The new dinosaur had three sharp horns and a bony hood on the top of her head. Levi knew the *Triceratops* was a plant-eating herbivore, but even so, this tank-sized reptile was a scary sight. Swallowing hard, he tried to stop his hands from shaking.

"Have you been p... picking on my friend?" he stammered. "I think you should stop."

The *Triceratops* growled again. "I haven't picked on *anyone*," she snorted. "I'm being bullied too!"

Levi and the *Edmontosaurus* approached the *Triceratops.* They joined her on a rocky ledge at the top of the slope. "I'm sorry to hear that," said Levi kindly. "We both know how it feels."

The *Edmontosaurus* nodded. "Who's *your* bully?" asked the duck-billed dinosaur.

The earth shook in reply, throwing Levi to the ground. The quaking grew worse, like giant footsteps coming closer. Something terrible was heading their way!

"Hurry!" yelled the *Triceratops*. "We have to hide!"

Levi dove behind a nearby boulder, but there were no rocks big enough to disguise a dinosaur. His friends had nowhere to hide! A moment later, a gigantic reptile stormed up the slope. Wider than a tank and taller than a truck, his long tail trailed behind him. Worst of all were his giant jaws crammed with razor-sharp teeth. This snarling dinosaur was a carnivore, for sure. He was a terrifying *Tyrannosaurus Rex!*

"What a silly beak," sneered the *T-Rex* to the *Edmontosaurus*. "And *you* are such a bonehead," he said, pointing to the *Triceratops*.

Crouched behind the rock, Levi's heart was thumping. The *T-Rex* was clearly his friends' bully. Levi had to stand up for them! He stepped out from behind the boulder. He hoped the *T-Rex* couldn't tell that his legs had turned to jelly.

"Stop it," said Levi, trying to sound fierce. "Imagine if someone was teasing *you*. How would that make you feel?" He covered his ears, expecting to hear the *T-Rex's* angry roar. But to his astonishment, the carnivore began to cry!

"When I was young," the *T-Rex* explained, "I was teased about my short arms. I decided I never wanted to feel that way again, so I became a bully myself. Now that I'm grown up, everyone runs away from me."

The *T-Rex's* tears splashed on the ground, and the two other dinosaurs *didn't* run away. Surprisingly, they rubbed their snouts on him! "What are you *doing*?" asked Levi.

"We're forgiving him," replied the *Triceratops*. "This is how dinosaurs make friends."

"You're our friend too," said the *Edmontosaurus*. "You may be a small creature, Levi, but you stood up to the biggest bully. That makes you amazingly brave."

Soon, the three reptiles were ready to head down the hill. The *Edmontosaurus* wasn't far from home, and he wanted to visit with his new dinosaur friends. As for Levi, he was worn out from all the climbing. His eyes were already closing, and his head was beginning to nod...

When Levi looked up, he was back on the bus. Aaron was snoozing beside him. Levi couldn't wait for his best friend to wake up. He had the most incredible dinosaur tale to tell!

#1

We were huge and heavy,
with horns or a beak.
Some were strong, while others were weak.
Long ago, we roamed the land.
What are we from a time so grand?

#2

Which word doesn't belong with the others?

Triceratops – Edmontosaurus
Tyrannosaurus – Stegosaurus

1. The Edmontosaurus was an herbivore that lived during the Late Cretaceous Period.
2. Tyrannosaurus Rex lived at the same time as Stegosaurus and often hunted them.
3. Triceratops had three horns and ate plants, not meat.

#3

Which number is the twist (the false one)?

CHAPTER 11

Meeting Amelia

When the school bell rang, Wren opened her eyes. She must have dozed off in class! She looked around, hoping nobody had noticed. She didn't want to be made fun of.

At school, Wren was cool and confident. Her friends thought she was funny, and she was always the leader in playground games. But secretly, she worried about what her friends thought, so Wren hid her fears behind her big personality. She kept on making jokes, so no one made fun of her.

To Wren's relief, she wasn't being laughed at. Her classmates were facing front and listening to Ms. Morales. "I'll see you all tomorrow," said her teacher. "I hope you have a safe journey home."

As soon as class was dismissed, Wren leaped to her feet. She pulled on her coat, grabbed her bag, and rushed out of the room. That afternoon, she *wasn't* taking the school bus home.

Outside, a bright red plane was parked in the schoolyard. Wren beamed at the gleaming aircraft. The sight of it took her breath away! The beautiful plane was a Lockheed Vega, built over a hundred years ago.

Wren had admired it once before at the National Air and Space Museum. Unlike modern planes, its nose had a propeller, and its wings sat high on top of the craft. In the middle of the wings was the pilot's cockpit. Wren couldn't *wait* to climb aboard.

"Wait up!" called her friend Hannah, running into the yard.

"What are you *doing*?" asked her friend Beau. "You've never flown before!"

Wren grinned. Once more, her friends were following her. "My dad is a pilot," she replied, "and I want to be just like him." She spun the propeller, which whirred around noisily. "Besides, don't you know who owned this plane? It was Amelia Earheart!"

Hannah and Beau both looked puzzled.

Wren sighed. "Amelia Earheart was a famous aviator. She was the first woman to fly solo across the Atlantic Ocean."

"If you fly *that* far, you'll miss school tomorrow," Hannah pointed out.

Wren folded her arms. "I'm not flying over the ocean," she said, "but I *am* going to be the first girl to fly home from school!"

She jumped into the cockpit and pulled on the pilot's goggles. Outside, Beau and Hannah were shouting for her to stop, but the sound of the engine drowned out their doubts. The powerful propeller thrust the airplane across the schoolyard. As the aircraft shook, Hannah gripped the control stick. Her Lockheed Vega was ready for takeoff!

The bright red plane zoomed into the clear blue sky. Wren was so excited! Peering out the windscreen, she watched her school shrink below. The yellow school buses waiting by the sidewalk looked like tiny toys. Her town got smaller by the second, till the people on the streets were no bigger than ants. But as Wren flew higher, her view became hazy. Soon, dark clouds surrounded the plane.

Now, Wren felt foolish thinking she could fly. She could push the pedals and pull the control stick to move the plane around, but that was useless if she couldn't see where she was going. She had totally lost her way!

Stuck on her own in the cockpit, Wren began to worry. If her flight failed, her friends wouldn't admire her anymore. Everyone would find out she wasn't cool or confident at all! She tried to ignore her doubts, but they seemed to grow even louder.

A moment later, the noisy propeller sputtered to a stop. As the plane plunged, Wren's heart pounded. "Help!" she yelled. "I'm falling from the sky!"

"Don't sweat it, gal," said a strange voice. "I've been in sticky spots like this before."

Wren's mouth dropped open. A short-haired lady was sitting beside her, wearing an aviator jacket. Wren had seen this woman in a black-and-white photograph. Amelia Earheart was her new co-pilot!

"There's ice on the wings," explained Amelia. "The same thing happened to me in 1932, on my trip across the Atlantic."

Wren wondered how Amelia was staying so calm. The plane was falling faster and faster! "Why did the ice appear?" she asked.

"Your doubts and fears froze the wings," replied Amelia. "You mustn't listen to those. If you follow your heart instead, you'll find your way home for sure."

Wren took a deep breath, letting her fear melt away. She held the control stick firmly and steered to one side.

Suddenly, the clouds cleared, and the plane was bathed in warm sunlight. To Wren's delight, the wings thawed, and the propeller started whirring!

A few minutes later, Wren made history. When the plane touched down onto her street, she became the first girl to fly home from school. Even better, she made a perfect landing!

Wren's neighbors ran out of their houses. Cameras flashed and music played as they greeted her with a ticker-tape parade. Coasting down the street, the red aircraft stopped right outside her house. Wren pulled off her goggles and waved to her dad. She knew she'd made him super-proud!

Wren had one last thing to do before she left the cockpit. "Thank you, Amelia," she said. "I couldn't have done that without you."

Weirdly, Amelia didn't reply. Turning in her seat, Wren discovered she was on her own. The famous aviator had vanished!

I flew alone across the sea,
A daring woman pilot—me!
With goggles on and engines loud,
Who am I that made the world proud?

#1

#2

Which word doesn't belong with the others?

Propeller – Lockheed Vega
Jet engine – Cockpit

1. Amelia Earhart was the first woman to fly solo across the Atlantic Ocean.
2. Amelia Earhart disappeared in 1937 while attempting to fly around the world.
3. Amelia Earhart's first famous flight was across the Pacific Ocean in 1925.

#3

Which number is the twist (the false one)?

CHAPTER 12

The Crystal Cave

In the dark tunnel, a distant glimmer caught Aaron's eye. Something ahead was sparkling in the beam from his flashlight.

"Did you see that?" he asked.

An echo was the only reply. Looking behind him, he realized that Levi wasn't there. Aaron was meant to be exploring with his best buddy, but as usual, he was rushing ahead.

Several steps behind him, Levi hurried around the corner. "This isn't a Little League game," he grumbled. "You don't have to win!"

"Sorry," said Aaron. "Let's stick together."

The boys scrambled through the shadowy passage. They slipped and tripped on the stones beneath their feet. Just as they reached the end of the tunnel, they both fell over.

"Ouch!" yelled Aaron, landing on his knees.

The boys had stumbled into a vast cavern. When Aaron raised his flashlight, jagged jewels glittered in the walls. Thousands of gemstones were fixed into the rock, bright green like emeralds, but the most impressive sight was in the center of the chamber.

Rising to the roof was the biggest crystal Aaron had ever seen! The green column seemed to glow from within. Its sides were uneven, yet shiny like ice. It was angular, awesome, and out of this world!

"Have we discovered... kryptonite?" asked Levi.

"No," replied Aaron. "This stone is called *elba-ite*."

The boys walked around the crystal column.

"I've seen elbaite before," explained Aaron, "in the Gem Hall at the museum. It's a kind of stone called *tourmaline*, which grows underground between volcanic rocks. When hot steam flows from the molten earth below, the vapor cools into crystals. Because of the different minerals in the earth, tourmaline comes in all kinds of colors."

"Woah!" said Levi. "You learned a *lot*. What should we do with our discovery?"

The crystal's green light was twinkling in Aaron's eye. It was hard to look away. "I think you mean *my* discovery," he replied. "It's going to make me mega-rich!"

Aaron rushed back into the tunnel, with Levi chasing after him. "I don't understand," said Levi. "How will it make you money?"

"People will pay to see this cave," replied Aaron. "I'll charge them five bucks each!"

The boys reached the top of the tunnel. Bursting out of the mountainside, they squinted in the bright daylight.

Aaron smirked at Levi. "Looks like we made it just in time!"

A passenger bus was parked near the foot of the mountain. A group of excited tourists climbed down and hurried in the direction of the cave. Guarding the tunnel entrance, Aaron could barely believe his luck. It was a dream come true!

Before long, Aaron's pockets were stuffed with cash. As the last of the tourists paid their entrance fee, he rubbed his hands with glee. "Think what I could buy with all these dollars," he said. "I'm gonna get a scooter, a game console, and that Green Goblin glider!"

"*Awesome*," sighed Levi, sounding a little sad. "Can I get something too?"

"Sure," replied Aaron. "I'll buy you a pack of baseball cards."

When the tourists left, Aaron was amazed at how much money he'd made, but it didn't stop him dreaming of making even *more*. A second bus arrived, even bigger than the first. The men who filed out were carrying pickaxes!

"What's going on?" whispered Levi. "This is like a scene from Snow White."

Levi was right. The men were miners! "We'd like to carve pieces of your crystal," said the miner at the head of the line.

"That's fine," replied Aaron, grinning again, "if you pay me *fifty* bucks each!"

As the miners entered the tunnel, Aaron shoved banknotes into his clothes.

"Why did you charge so much?" asked Levi. "Don't you think that's a little greedy?"

Before Aaron could answer, a sickening sound echoed up the tunnel. The two boys turned slowly and stared into the shadows. From deep in the cave came the awful *clang* of metal striking stone. Aaron felt like every strike was breaking him from a spell.

"I've made a mistake," he moaned. "Those miners will destroy the beautiful elbaite!"

Panicking, Aaron ran into the darkness, quickly followed by Levi. When the boys staggered into the cave, they both gasped in horror.

At the center of the chamber, the green crystal was dull and not glowing anymore. The brilliant gemstone had been damaged by the miners' heavy blows. As the men chipped away, the crystal column *cracked*! The ground trembled, the walls split, and the cave began to shake.

"We have to leave," shouted Aaron. "This place is going to collapse!"

Right then, the roof cracked too, and rocks started to rain down on their heads. Aaron and Levi fled the cave, dodging the deadly stones. The ground was uneven, and the narrow tunnel was full of frightened miners. Caught in the chaos, Aaron tripped. His dollars flew into the air!

"Oh no!" he groaned. "I've lost all my money."

Levi reached the top of the tunnel first. When he heard Aaron cry out, he turned around and ran back to rescue his friend. He grabbed Aaron by the hand and pulled him toward the light. The boys escaped just as the tunnel collapsed.

KA-BOOM!

When the dust settled, Aaron looked guiltily at his friend. "You're right," he said, "I was greedy. Now, no one else can enjoy the crystal cave."

"You might not be rich anymore," said Levi, "but I reckon you learned a valuable lesson."

Aaron watched the miners getting back on their bus. Reaching deep into his pocket, he pulled out one crumpled banknote.

"Hey," he said, "I didn't lose *all* my money. Lucky for us, I have enough for our bus fare home!"

I sparkle bright, both green and red.
I grow in rocks beneath Earth's bed.
Formed by heat and steam below,
What am I that shines and glows?

#1

#2

Which word doesn't belong with the others?

Quartz – Tourmaline
Diamond – Marble

1. Elbaite, a type of tourmaline, is always blue and never found in green or pink.
2. Tourmaline crystals can be found in many colors, depending on the minerals in the ground.
3. Crystals grow when gases and steam from hot magma slowly cool and harden underground.

#3

Which number is the twist (the false one)?

CHAPTER 13

The Plundering Pirates

Sebastian didn't know how he'd gotten here. He was teetering at the end of a long plank! It had always been his dream to see a pirate ship someday. His favorite stories of all were the ones about buried treasure. But now that his dream had come true, Sebastian wished it hadn't. Seeing a ship from the end of a plank wasn't *exactly* what he'd imagined.

The pirate captain walked along the plank, making it wobble even more. To Sebastian's surprise, the captain looked a lot like Principal Nelson. Aside from his eyepatch, there was one key difference: Captain Nelson had a crab claw instead of a hand!

"Time for you to dive," snarled the captain, waving his claw in Sebastian's face.

"Wait!" shouted Sebastian, trying to buy some time. "How do you pick your nose?"

At the other end of the plank, the galleon's crew hooted with laughter. But when Captain Nelson glared at them, the terrified pirates went silent. "You're funny, kid," the captain sneered, "but there's a time and place for jokes."

Sebastian gulped. He was sure that *Principal* Nelson had said that to him once. He almost wished he was back in the principal's office. Right now, the crabby captain was breathing all over his face.

"There's treasure in Coral Bay," explained the captain, "and I want *you* to go get it. When we pirates dive to find the gold, the mermaids stop us with their magical powers." A tear rolled down his hairy cheek. "Those mermaids have transformed so many of my crew."

Sebastian peered at the pirates scrubbing the deck. One man was mopping the ship with his flippers. Another was washing the wood with his whale-like tail. A third pirate was having trouble with his tentacles. The poor sucker was sliding around in circles!

Sebastian looked down at the turquoise water sparkling below him. Although Coral Bay looked beautiful, he didn't want to dive to his doom. All at once, his legs began to wobble. The impatient pirate captain was bouncing on the plank!

"Are you sure you want *me* to go?" asked Sebastian. "That octopus pirate could carry eight times more treasure."

"Step on it!" snarled Captain Nelson, shoving him overboard. "And make sure you grab as much gold as you can."

SPLASH!

Water rushed up Sebastian's nose, and the world turned green-blue. The ocean was cool and crystal clear. Sebastian was thankful that he couldn't see any sign of mermaids. Scanning the area, he wondered if Captain Nelson had been lying. There was no gold to be seen either!

Sebastian swam toward the seabed, trying hard to hold his breath. Grabbing hold of a rock, he decided to wait. Maybe the pirates would sail away if he stayed underwater.

When something touched Sebastian's shoulder, his whole body shuddered. Suddenly, a woman's hand covered his mouth! He waited for his skin to turn scaly or his nose to grow long like a swordfish. But when the hand was removed, Sebastian hadn't been transformed. Instead, he discovered he could breathe underwater!

"Hello, Sebastian," said a gentle voice.

Behind him was a school of mermaids, floating in the ocean. Their tails shimmered in the light shining down from the surface. The seven mermaids each had long hair in colors of the rainbow. Best of all were their friendly smiles. The mermaids didn't seem mad at all!

"Hello," replied Sebastian. "Aren't you going to give me gills or something?"

He was surprised to hear his own voice. It sounded further away somehow.

The mermaid with green hair shook her head. "No," she replied. "We know you are a good boy at heart."

Sebastian smirked. "You should tell my principal."

"My name is Samphira," said the mermaid, "and these are my sisters. Please follow us. We have something to show you."

As the mermaids flipped their tails, Sebastian kicked as hard as he could. He followed them over the ocean floor, wondering where they were going. Soon, a beautiful city appeared before his eyes. It nearly took his magical breath away!

Swimming closer, Sebastian realized that the city was a reef. He'd seen one on display in the Ocean Hall at the museum. The reef was made of precious coral, one of the world's natural wonders. Built by tiny creatures called polyps, it was a rainbow of colors!

When Sebastian arrived at the reef, a shoal of fish swam past him. He smiled at two turtles peering from their shells and waved at a herd of floating seahorses. To his great delight, the coral reef was teeming with life!

The mermaid sisters were helping to mend the reef. "The colony is home to thousands of creatures," said Samphira. "This reef is the *real* treasure of Coral Bay."

Sebastian nodded. "It's way more valuable than gold. Coral reefs protect the seashore by slowing down big waves."

"You're right," replied Samphira, "but the diving pirates are damaging the reef."

Sebastian felt sad. His dream of buried treasure had turned into something more serious. The ocean creatures were working together, while the greedy pirates only thought about themselves. But unlike the mermaids, Sebastian didn't have magical powers. What could he do to save the rainbow reef?

"I've got the answer!" he declared. "It's right there in front of me!"

Not long after, a glimmering arch shot out of the turquoise water. Rising high into the sky, it curved back down to the distant horizon. Beneath the waves, Sebastian smiled at the magical sight. The mermaid sisters had created a rainbow!

He watched as the pirate crew pulled up their anchor. Searching for the gold at the end of the rainbow, they sailed away from Coral Bay.

But Sebastian's delight quickly turned to panic. "Hang on," he said, "I need a ride home!"

Sebastian swam desperately after the ship. At that moment, he *wished* he had flippers.

A distant voice dragged him out of the ocean.

"Wake *up*," said his best friend, Beau. "You're hitting me in the face!"

I sail the seas both near and far,
With a treasure chest or a Jolly Roger star.
I search for gold where X marks the spot,
Who am I, with a map and a plot?

#1

Which word doesn't belong with the others?

#2

Coral – Polyps – Reef – Eyepatch

1. Coral reefs are built by tiny animals called polyps.
2. Pirates often buried their treasure on desert islands.
3. Coral reefs help protect shorelines from big waves.

#3

Which number is the twist (the false one)?

CHAPTER 14

The Golden Spike

A BUMPY MOTION woke Wyatt from his snooze. It seemed the sleepy school bus had picked up some speed! Lifting the wide brim of his Stetson, he looked at the view outside. Massive, rust-colored mountains were rushing past the window.

Wyatt wasn't sitting on the school bus anymore. He was traveling on a train through the Wild West!

Winding down the window, Wyatt looked along the carriages. Up ahead, the train's engine was puffing across the plain. Pumping pistons powered by steam were turning the big, red wheels.

The locomotive's famous name was painted in gold on the side. Wyatt had seen the gleaming *Jupiter* in the Museum of American History. But now, the dusty train was racing along the rails.

FA-WOOO!

Hearing a shrieking whistle, Wyatt leaped from his seat. It sounded like the steam engine was in terrible trouble! Wyatt half expected to hear his teacher telling him to sit down. In class, he was often told off for being too wild. Wyatt didn't know *why* he found it so hard to sit still.

He ran through the carriages, almost tripping on his big cowboy boots. At the end of the front carriage, the warm, desert wind rushed into his face. Holding his hat, he jumped onto the *Jupiter's* locomotive, then leaped down into the cab.

"Howdy," said Wyatt, lifting the brim of his hat.

"Thank g... goodness y'all are here," stammered the engineer. He sounded terrified.

The engineer explained that the *Jupiter* was steaming along the Central Pacific Railroad to a place called Promontory Summit. There, the track met the Union Pacific Railroad, where the two would soon be joined with a golden spike. For the first time in American history, passengers would be able to travel right across the continent!

Wyatt listened to the man without growing restless. History was a subject he *enjoyed*. "Why do you sound so scared?" asked Wyatt.

JUPITE

The engineer pointed a trembling finger across the desert. "Because that train is approaching too f… fast," he replied. "Ah've tried whistlin', but it won't slow down!"

Wyatt peered through the wiggly heat waves rising from the desert. In the distance, he could see another locomotive. The golden number plate on its nose was glinting in the sun.

"That's *No. 119*," explained the panicked engineer. "It's heading toward us on the other railroad. If it don't slow down, we're both gonna crash!" He took a white handkerchief from his pocket and mopped the soot off his face. "Ah thought y'all had come to save me!"

Wyatt was confused. "You keep saying *y'all*, but I'm the only one here!"

The engineer looked just as puzzled. "B… but you're Wyatt," he stammered, "the famous Wild Cowboy. Surely Bolo is back there in the cattle cars?"

Suddenly, what the engineer was saying made sense.

"Of *course*," declared Wyatt, "I couldn't forget Bolo. He's the Fastest Horse in the West!"

Putting two fingers into his mouth, Wyatt whistled. It was almost as loud as the shrieking train! A second later, a golden stallion galloped into view. The beautiful horse had a flowing mane the color of flame. He ran beside the train without getting breathless!

"Don't worry," said Wyatt to the engineer. "Bolo and I will stop that train."

He jumped off the *Jupiter* and onto Bolo's back. With a squeeze of his spurs, the two of them raced across the dusty plain. "It's another adventure for us both!" declared Bolo. "I'm glad you're back in the saddle."

"Hold your horses," replied Wyatt. "I didn't know you could speak!"

Bolo brayed with laughter. "Of course I can," he answered. "Riding in silence is boring!"

As Bolo's hooves sped to a blur, Wyatt gripped his hat. The distant train was growing bigger every moment! They raced past a grassy patch of desert where some men were gathering next to the iron rails. One man held a hammer and a large, golden nail. This was where the railroads were going to be joined! But first, the oncoming train had to be stopped. Otherwise, the meeting would end in disaster.

When Wyatt and Bolo reached the *No. 119*, the air was thick with smoke. Its pistons were pounding, and the engine was screaming. The runaway train was out of control! Standing up in his saddle, Wyatt almost lost his balance, but with one wild leap, he landed on the locomotive.

To Wyatt's horror, the train's engineer was unconscious in the cab. "What do I do?" he yelled above the noise. "How do I stop the train?"

"Pull the steam brake lever!" replied Bolo, galloping beside the train.

Wyatt pulled the lever with all his strength. As the engine braked suddenly, its wheels *screeched.* Wyatt could see the *Jupiter* growing closer, and the frightened, white eyes of its engineer. Wyatt screwed his own eyes shut. The trains were going to crash!

When nothing happened, Wyatt peeked out from underneath his Stetson. To his amazement, the *No. 119* had stopped *just* in time! The two locomotives were nearly nose to nose, with the crowd squeezed between them. The golden spike was hammered into the ground, and the cheering men threw their hats into the air.

Whooping with joy, Wyatt jumped off the train. He smiled at Bolo and stroked his glossy coat. "We did it, boy!" he declared. "We saved the day! And no one told me to sit down once."

“Of course they didn’t,” replied the horse. “If you weren’t so wild, we couldn’t have stopped that train.”

Wyatt beamed at Bolo. “So, my energy is really a superpower?” he asked.

“Sure,” said Bolo, braying with laughter. “All the best cowboys are full of beans!”

#1

I travel on rails, puffing clouds in the sky,
With pistons that pump as the wheels roll by.
I carried folks west, both steady and fast.
What am I, built in the past?

#2

Which word doesn't belong with the others?

Jupiter – No. 119
Golden Spike – Stetson

1. The "Golden Spike" marked the joining of the Central Pacific and Union Pacific railroads in 1869.
2. After the railroads were joined, it became possible to travel across the United States in less than a week.
3. The Golden Spike was used to hold the railroad tracks together forever.

#3

Which number is the twist (the false one)?

CHAPTER 15

The Brilliant Blue Balloon

At the National Air and Space Museum, Blue raced past the Milestones of Flight. As she ran beneath a rocket and spun around a satellite, she imagined she was blasting off to the stars. The museum even had a super-cool rover that once traveled across Mars! Hurrying past the exhibits, Blue's brain raced with excitement. She didn't have time to read the signs or listen to a guide. She was here for speed, explosions, and action.

Rushing around a corner, Blue skidded to a halt. Her classmates were staring at a massive balloon made from fabric and rope. It hung from the ceiling like a saggy potato . . . except it was covered with faded blue paint.

"Why's this balloon so famous?" she muttered. "Did it *bore* someone to death?"

Adam turned around. "This balloon made the first manned flight," he replied excitedly. "Imagine what *that* must have felt like!"

Blue's jaw almost fell to the floor. "*This* balloon?" she replied. "No way."

She rolled her eyes. The faded, fabric potato was seriously unimpressive. But if Adam *was* right as usual, it had been the first to carry people off the ground. When her classmates walked away, Blue decided to stay behind. Creeping closer, she paused to read a golden plaque. Invented by the Montgolfier Brothers, this hot air balloon had made the first successful flight in 1783.

"Whoa," Blue said, raising her eyebrows, "it's even older than my dad."

As she reached up to touch the balloon, a gust of wind blew her hair into her face. Brushing it aside, her eyes went wide. The air was smoky, the sky was bright—and she was rising off the ground inside a basket! Looking up, Blue was shocked to see the same balloon as before. But now, its paint was fresh, and its silky fabric was decorated with golden swirls and suns. As the basket swung from side to side, Blue's belly did the same. The jerky motion wasn't as fun as riding a roller coaster. To make things worse, someone was shouting at her in French.

"Vous n'êtes pas le pilote!" a boy with long hair and a frilly shirt yelled.

"What?" Blue replied rudely. "Can't you see I'm busy holding on for dear life?"

The boy stepped closer. "Pas le pilote!" he repeated. "And even worse, you is English!"

"I'm *American*," Blue replied, relieved that the language barrier was broken.

Secretly, she wished she'd listened more in her history lessons. Were the USA and France on friendly terms in 1783? But when something whizzed past her ear, Blue had bigger things to worry about. Someone was firing at the balloon! Ducking beside the boy, she peered over the edge of the basket. Down below, men on horseback galloped through the grounds of a grand chateau. Some of the blue-coated soldiers barked orders. The others waved their swords at the balloon. When Blue saw a regiment reloading a cannon, she froze with fear. The massive barrel was pointing in her direction!

"This is crazy!" she hissed to the boy. "*Who* are you, *why* are we here, and *what* are they doing down there?"

"I am called Jean-François," the boy began. "Enchantée, mademoiselle."

When he tried to kiss her hand, Blue snatched it away. "We haven't got time for that," she protested, hoping he didn't notice her blush. "Why are they *firing* at us?"

BANG!

A cannonball ripped past, reeking of gunpowder. As Blue ducked again, it struck the balloon, tearing a hole in the delicate fabric. Jean-François leaped onto his leather-booted feet. Wrestling with a rope to turn the balloon, his face was a picture of panic.

"We must 'ead over the mountains!" he declared. "Those soldiers think we is spies."

"You're a *spy*?" Blue shouted. "Then *why* are you traveling in a giant blue balloon?"

"I am not a spy," the boy replied, "but it does not matter. If those men strike us again, we will *both* be on the ropes!"

Blue yanked another rope, helping Jean-François to steer the torn balloon. As it drifted beyond the range of the soldiers, she breathed a sigh of relief. With every moment, the safety of the mountains grew closer.

"Uh-oh," the boy groaned, "we are much too low. In fact, we are on a collision course!"

Blue's brain raced into action. "Then we need to lighten our load," she realized. "Something on board is dragging us down!" Leaning the basket to one side, she began tossing out heavy, metal equipment. "I mean, who brings a brass box on board a balloon?"

"Non!" Jean-François yelled. "Not my weather reader!

I need it to complete my mission."

Blue dropped the box inside the basket. Lifting the lid, she peered at its spinning dials. "You're a *scientist*!" she said. "The way you're dressed, I would've guessed a pirate."

With a lighter basket, the balloon rose faster and higher. To the delight of its passengers, it narrowly missed the mountains. But in the valley beyond, the sky was blacker than ink.

"I'm *not* a scientist," Blue muttered, "but to me, that looks like a storm."

"Pas de problème," the boy replied, "we will float out of 'ere in no time!"

Jean-François turned up the fuel in the gas-powered burner. At the same time, the balloon tore again. As heat leaked out through the wide gash, the flame dimmed, and the basket sank. Now, there was no way to avoid the oncoming storm.

While lightning flashed and thunder cracked, the balloon shuddered. Surrounded by the mighty weather, Blue felt small and scared. Stuck in the sky, she wasn't protected by a metal spacecraft. Her balloon didn't have a powerful rocket, or even a propeller to push it away.

The crazy people who'd made the first flight had done something risky . . . and very brave.

Suddenly, the brass box at her feet started sparking. When Blue opened its lid, the dials were whirring around in a blur.

"Ah non!" Jean-François cried out with tears in his eyes. "My weather reader is overloaded. Because of the thunderstorm, the box is going to shatter. The pressure is just too great!"

"Not for me, it isn't!" Blue declared.

Glad for the distraction, she sprang into action again. Pulling off her sweater, she wrapped it around the weather reader. To Jean-François's delight, she saved it from shattering.

"I love Americans!" the boy cheered. "I could kiss you on the cheek."

"I'd rather you didn't," Blue replied, "but I'm happy I saved the mission."

Suddenly, a bolt of lightning struck the basket. For a second, the world went white. When the light faded, Blue was amazed. She was standing in the museum again, and her sweater smelled of smoke. The saggy balloon looked the same—including the tear on its side—but when she glanced down, Blue noticed a new line engraved on the golden plaque.

"Recovered after lightning storm, 1783," she read. *"Pilot unknown."*

Jasmine ran around the corner, searching for her classmate. "It's just a balloon," she said, giggling at Blue's astonished expression.

Blue now knew why the brilliant balloon had a prized place in history. It was human *curiosity*, not power, that had led to the discovery of flight. Before propellers, rockets, and jets, someone had looked at the sky and dared to try.

"It's not *just* a balloon," Blue replied. "It's way more thrilling than that."

#1

I rise without wings. I float without sound.
A basket below, I lift off the ground.
Long before rockets, before airplanes flew,
What carried the first
brave passengers too?

#2

Which word doesn't belong with the others?

Silk Fabric – Rope Netting
Burner Flame – Propeller

1. The Montgolfier balloon was steered easily using a wooden wheel like a ship's rudder.
2. The Montgolfier Brothers first tested their balloon with animals before flying humans.
3. Their hot air balloon worked because heated air is lighter than the cooler air outside.

#3

Which number is the twist (the false one)?

CHAPTER 16

Potomac Shark Attack!

Brooke frowned at her lunch with confusion. She was sure she'd eaten these tuna sandwiches before. It was hard to forget the prehistoric shark that had hung overhead while she chewed her food. In the Museum of Natural History, the massive creature was suspended above the dining area. Sitting beneath the monstrous megalodon, Brooke had felt like *she* might be lunch!

Taking a bite, Brooke looked out across West Potomac Park. She and her classmates were sitting on the grass, gazing at the river that ran through Washington, DC. Pausing mid-mouthful, she turned to her classmate Stella. "Are you *sure* we haven't eaten lunch already?"

Stella gave her a funny look. "Of *course*," she replied, "I think I would remember."

The problem was that Brooke *did* remember. Although her friend sounded confident, Brooke was sure *she* was right. But as usual, Brooke decided to stay silent. She always avoided disagreements when possible. If she wanted to stay popular at school, she couldn't fall out with anyone, so Brooke never disagreed with her friends—even when she knew they were wrong.

FWOOOSH!

Suddenly, the river rose into a towering fountain. A giant shark burst out of the water, displaying its sharp, shovel-sized teeth. It landed on the grass with a heavy *thump*, soaking Brooke and all her classmates. As her tuna sandwich turned to fishy mush, her legs turned to jelly. Why was a prehistoric predator living in the Potomac?

"It's a *megalosaurus*!" Stella screamed, scrambling away from the riverbank.

As she followed Stella, Brooke didn't correct her friend. She knew that the megalodon once lived in Chesapeake Bay, from where it could easily swim upriver, but that had been millions of years ago. Right now, the shark attacking the capital didn't look very extinct!

Longer than a bowling lane, the megalodon thrashed around on the grass. As it gnashed its gaping jaws, Brooke gulped. The shark's mouth was wide enough to fit two adults inside.

"Stop staring!" Stella yelled. "We have to get outta here!"

Stella fled with the other fourth graders who were stumbling over the grass. But for some reason, Brooke slowed down. The megalodon hadn't moved an inch farther from the river.

"Wait a moment," she realized, "that shark isn't attacking anyone."

WhapWhapWhapWhap!

Brooke's voice was drowned out by whirring rotor blades. To her astonishment, a long line of helicopters flew across the Potomac. Brooke guessed they had come from the Pentagon, the base of Washington's military commanders. Tilting her head back, she watched them land beside the Lincoln Memorial. It was like a scene from the action movies her brothers always chose. While the helicopters' blades were still spinning, soldiers jumped out beside the famous monument. Carrying weapons, the men and women ran toward the park.

Brooke caught up to her classmates, who were watching the soldiers approach. "What are you all staring at?" she asked.

"Him!" Harris replied, pointing ahead.

With a shaven head and big muscles, the soldiers' commander was leading the way. Dressed in fatigues, he didn't look tired at all. The man striding toward them was Coach Judge!

"I *knew* it!" Yuki whispered. "I always said he was a Marine."

It was really Brooke who had started that rumor. But once again, she didn't speak up. By now, the soldiers had surrounded the students. Some of them marched off to secure the park, while others escorted the fourth graders to safety. As a Marine dragged her away from the river, Brooke felt torn.

"Stop!" she shouted. "That shark in the park isn't a threat. Something *else* is going on!"

Turning around, Commander Judge frowned in her direction. "You don't know that," he disagreed, "so keep your mouth shut. I'm gonna show that monster who's boss!" He marched back toward his helicopter. "Get ready for takeoff!" he barked into his walkie-talkie.

Biting her lip, Brooke didn't protest. Getting scolded by Commander Judge was the last thing she wanted, but she was sure that the shark was *already* in trouble. The feeling was super strong! Slipping free of the soldier's grip, she chased the commander onto his chopper. A second later, it hovered off the ground.

"What are you doing?" Stella shrieked from the ground below.

Rising into the sky, Brooke smiled at Stella. "I'm speaking up for myself!"

Commander Judge was astounded to see Brooke on board. His eyes almost bulged out of their sockets. "I already said you were wrong," he barked. "Why don't you follow orders?"

But as the aircraft rose above the river, the truth was revealed. Below the water, Brooke saw four megalodon pups. They were trapped beneath a fallen tree!

"Of course!" she exclaimed. "Unlike modern sharks, the megalodon looked after its own young. Instead of leaving their babies behind, they raised them in shallo-w-water nurseries."

"Those *can't* be babies," the commander spat. "Each one is the size of a car!"

"You're *wrong*," Brooke replied, "and they need our help. Why else is the megalodon mother trying to get our attention?"

For a moment, Brooke and Commander Judge said nothing. They were both surprised she had been so bold. After that, the commander fastened a harness around her waist.

"You *might* be right," the man admitted. "It's time to put your belief to the test."

Before Brooke knew it, she was being lowered from the aircraft on a scarily thin rope. She felt so afraid. She couldn't decide what was worse: Hanging from a helicopter high in the air or dangling like bait above a prehistoric shark. As her feet got closer to the thrashing creature, Brooke tried not to stare down its deep, black throat. If she was right, the shark wouldn't attack. But if she was wrong, she'd be its afternoon snack!

The helicopter's winch lowered Brooke to the water, where she could reach the fallen tree. As she attached a hook to one of its branches, the megalodon mother watched with glassy, black eyes. Thankfully, the shark didn't take a bite. When Brooke pointed toward the sky, the rope lifted. Slowly, the tree was pulled to one side—freeing the oversized pups!

As Brooke was pulled on board the helicopter, the megalodon slid back into the Potomac. The shark family swam away, vanishing into the depths. Across the park, Brooke's ant-sized classmates cheered. When a soldier removed her harness, she collapsed with relief.

"You were right!" Commander Judge said. "You should speak up more often."

"I *will*," Brooke promised with an exhausted yawn. "But first, I'd like to go down again."

I lived in the ocean. My teeth were so wide,
As big as shovels, set side by side.
Longer than buses, I gave fish a fright—
Which giant shark once ruled the bite?

#1

#2

Which word doesn't belong with the others?

Megalodon – Great White
Hammerhead – Mosasaur

1. Most megalodon "fossils" are teeth because sharks have skeletons made mostly of cartilage.
2. Scientists think megalodon mothers used warm, shallow nurseries to protect their pups.
3. Museums often display full megalodon skeletons made from original bones found together.

#3

Which number is the twist (the false one)?

CHAPTER 17

The Runaway Trolley Problem

Dylan's nap was rudely interrupted by frightened screams. A moment later, a bump in the road bounced him wide awake. Dylan discovered he was dressed in a hat and a button-down vest. Most surprising was his neat red tie. He'd always been able to talk his way out of wearing a tie in the past.

"This is a uniform," Dylan groaned. "That means I have a *job*!"

Dylan realized he was riding inside an old electric streetcar. He'd seen one at the Museum of African American History. Painted yellow, the Capital Traction tram had trundled around Washington, DC, in the early twentieth century. Just like this trolley, it was built from wood and had space for up to sixty passengers. Dylan hadn't heard about Washington trolleys before, which were powered by electrical wires in the tracks. He'd only ever seen the San Francisco streetcars, which connected to overhead cables. In fact, the street outside looked a lot like the famously sloping city. Maybe that explained why Dylan's trolley was rolling downhill!

"Help us!" a woman yelled into his ear. "This streetcar is out of control!"

A trembling man shook Dylan by the shoulders. "You're the conductor. *Do* something!"

Whirling around, Dylan began to panic. Whenever he had a problem at school, someone else usually solved it. He didn't prepare for his teacher's quizzes, since he could rely on his classmates for the answers. And when all else failed, Dylan relied on his charm. Making excuses was his favorite subject!

To Dylan's dismay, the trolley sped up. Outside, the sloping street was becoming a blur. As he ran to the front of the carriage, he found it hard to stay on his feet. He stumbled out to the open-air section where the terrified passengers gripped onto poles.

"I know it's rush hour," an old lady wailed, "but I didn't expect a white-knuckle ride!"

Thankfully, Dylan spotted someone else wearing the same uniform. Even better, he was a grown-up.

"You look *super* smart," Dylan began. "Do you know how to stop this streetcar?"

The pale man turned around. Beads of sweat rolled down his face.

"I'm Powell," he replied, "the gripman who operates the trolley." His bottom lip began to wobble. "But I can't get it to stop!"

As the trolley rolled around a corner, the passengers screamed like a theme park crowd. Frantically, Powell pressed a pedal with his foot. When nothing happened, he started to cry. It seemed the gripman was losing his grip!

"The wheel brakes have failed!" Powell wailed. "I'll have to try the track brakes."

Reaching out to a large lever, he yanked it toward him. Expecting a sudden brake, Dylan grabbed the nearest pole. Instead, the lever broke off in Powell's hand, and the runaway trolley continued to pick up speed.

The streetcar careened around another corner. Seeing an intersection ahead, Powell turned even paler. He crumpled into a heap almost in slow motion. The frightened gripman had fainted—leaving Dylan in charge! As the trolley raced over the junction, Dylan closed

303
303
CAPI

his eyes. Luckily, the lights had only just turned red. even so, the waiting traffic didn't sound pleased.

Honk! Hoooooonk!

According to the signs, the trolley was speeding down Hyde Street. Hurrying inside, Dylan wished *he* could hide too, but the carriage's benches were stuffed with passengers.

"I can't afford to crash," a man clutching a crystal vase said.

"Please save us all!" a woman carrying a tank full of fish cried.

Another man was handcuffed to a silver briefcase. "The *world* is relying on you," he declared. "I must deliver these top-secret codes!"

Dylan gulped again. The situation was getting more serious by the second. Usually, he had a way with words, but as the panicking passengers pleaded, he didn't know what to say.

"I'm only n-nine," he stammered. "Maybe one of you fine people could help me?"

The adults didn't fall for Dylan's charm. In fact, they were less than impressed. A red-faced man rose to his feet. His mustache quivered, just like Dylan's dad's did when he was mad. "Are you unprepared for this test?" he asked, jabbing his finger at Dylan's face. "Why don't you take your studies more seriously?"

A scowling baby pulled out her pacifier. "You can't talk your way out of *this* problem!"

Backing away, Dylan fell onto his bottom. The street had grown even steeper, and the runaway trolley was hurtling down the slope! Glancing over his shoulder, Dylan gasped. He could now see San Francisco Bay, sparkling in the distance like a bright blue doom. As his heart pounded, Dylan scrambled beneath the benches. He pushed past the briefcase, fish tank, and stroller, desperate to find *something* that could help him.

Discovering a dusty book, Dylan whooped with joy. "It's the trolley's operation manual!"

But as he flicked through the thick volume, his dread returned. Reading a book felt like homework. He'd been able to get away without doing homework for *ages*.

Hastily, he tried to cram as much information as possible. The bay below was growing bigger and bigger. In less than a minute, he'd be facing a watery fate! The trolley shot past Lombard Street, where the road twisted and turned like a snake, but Dylan didn't stop to see the sights. He *had* to find the emergency brake.

With a few seconds left, Dylan turned another page. He read about a red lever hidden near the gripman. Bursting outside, Dylan leaped over Powell who was now half awake. Grabbing hold of the red lever, he pulled it with all his might.

"Oh no," Dylan moaned, "we won't slow down in time!"

Screeeeeeeeeech!

As the streetcar slid to the bottom of the hill, sparks flew from its wheels. Holding his breath, Dylan could hardly bear to watch. But to his amazement, the trolley curved around the corner . . . and came to a halt at the very end of the line!

Powell patted him on the shoulder. "Thanks for helping me out! I really needed a break."

Dylan shook his head. "I don't deserve any thanks. I only barely passed my test."

The dazed passengers staggered off the trolley, clutching their precious belongings. Sadly, the man with the priceless vase tripped on the stroller and dropped it, smashing it to pieces. Meanwhile, Dylan beat a hasty retreat, rushing into a park with a view over the bay.

Across the water, Alcatraz prison was perched on its

rocky island. Shuddering, Dylan pulled off his hat and vest. "I hope no one sends me to jail for being unprepared," he said.

Deciding to keep a low profile, Dylan laid on the grass. Closing his eyes, he pretended to fall asleep. Today had been a narrow escape, which he didn't want to repeat. In the future, he would take his studies a lot more seriously.

#1

I roll on tracks, not on the street,
With seats inside for folks to meet.
Powered by wires, I hum and sway—
What kind of ride takes you this way?

#2

Which word doesn't belong with the others?

Trolley – Cable car – Subway – Airplane

#3

1. Early Washington, DC, trolleys used electric power from wires hidden beneath the street.
2. All trolleys in the early 1900s could fly short distances when going downhill.
3. San Francisco's famous streetcars are pulled along by a moving underground cable.

Which number is the twist (the false one)?

CHAPTER 18

Fright at the Museum

MATEO STRUGGLED to open his eyes. It was hard working the night shift as a museum security guard. It was even harder when you were only eight! Mateo was used to his eyelids feeling heavy. He often fell asleep in math class on Monday mornings. Mateo believed he didn't have much choice in the matter. He *had* to stay up late to watch his favorite scary movies.

As he patrolled the dark hallway, Mateo wasn't having fun. Walking through the natural history museum felt more like a nightmare! In the shadowy main hall, Mateo's imagination ran wild. Hearing a noise, he shone his flashlight at Henry the Elephant. He was *sure* the eleven-ton animal had just twitched his trunk.

"Hello!" said a voice, making him jump.

Mateo's thumping heart almost leaped out of his chest! To his relief, he realized the voice was coming from his walkie talkie. "I'm here," he answered. "Is everything okay, boss?"

"It is *now*," crackled the voice. "I'm checking you're not asleep on the job!"

Mateo sighed. It wasn't his fault he was always so tired. "I'm keeping my eyes open," he replied. "Nothing is going missing tonight."

Smash!

The distant sound made Mateo shudder. He pointed his flashlight up toward the second floor. The noise had come from the Hall of Gems! Climbing the stairs, Mateo grew more nervous with every step. Who *else* was creeping around the museum in the dead of night? If he bumped into someone scary, he would surely die of fright.

When he reached the second floor, Mateo turned left, shining his flashlight into the gem gallery. The room sparkled in brilliant colors. Then his shoe *crunched* on some broken glass, and he saw that a display case had been smashed! Mateo gaped at the jagged hole in horror. He knew the case should contain the famous Carmen Lúcia Ruby. One of the largest rubies in the world, the gemstone was set in a platinum ring.

Mateo waved his flashlight around in panic. The ruby was *nowhere* to be seen.

"Report, please," crackled his walkie talkie.

"Everything's fine," lied Mateo. "It's all completely Carmen." A cold bead of sweat ran down his head. "I mean, completely *calm*."

"Glad to hear it," replied his boss. "If anything is stolen, *you'll* be to blame."

Mateo's eyes filled with water. He bit his lip to fight back the tears. If he didn't find the ruby, he'd be in big trouble. But if he *did* track it down, he'd have to face the thief!

He decided to try anyway. Leaving the gem gallery, he headed into the Bone Hall. Right away, he wondered if he'd made the right choice. The long room was stuffed with creepy skeletons!

Mateo hurried past the dog, camel, and monkey bones. Even though they had no eyes, he could feel the creatures watching from the shadows. He rushed beneath a whale's giant rib cage, a shiver traveling down his spine.

Mateo saw a glint of red out the corner of his eye. It was coming from the far end of the hall! Shining his flashlight, Mateo frowned. That part of the museum was home to the Egyptian mummies.

The "Eternal Life" exhibit was deathly quiet. Mateo could only hear his echoing footsteps. He shone his flashlight on the colorful coffins covered in hieroglyphics. The Ancient Egyptians believed these containers carried their loved ones to the afterlife.

Mateo knew it wasn't only people who'd been wrapped in bandages. He'd discovered on his school trip that animals were mummified too! Special creatures, like cats and snakes, joined humans on their journeys.

Although Mateo knew a little about mummies, he had a surprise in store. Peering below a coffin, he gasped in astonishment. A mummified cat was holding the ruby in its mouth. At last, he'd caught the culprit!

Mateo wondered if the cat burglar could understand English. "Hey, kitty," he said, "can I have my ruby back? Wouldn't you like some Friskies instead?"
Creeeeeeeeak!

The coffin lid opened slowly. Scrambling backward, Mateo *screamed*! A bandaged man sat up in the coffin. He stared at the boy with sunken eyes. Mateo was way too frightened to speak. This was the worst nightmare ever!

To Mateo's relief, the mummy was very polite. "Forgive me, young man," he said, "I hope I didn't frighten you." He coughed to clear the dust from his throat. "My name is Minister Cox. What are you doing up so late?"

"I'm the night watchman," explained Mateo, climbing to his feet.

Minister Cox shook his head. "Good gracious," he replied, "you're so young! You should be asleep at this time of night."

Mateo looked down. "That's what my teacher keeps telling me."

"Sleep is important," replied the mummy. "I've been doing it for two thousand years!"

Suddenly, the mummified cat jumped onto the coffin. Dropping the ruby into her master's hands, she meowed proudly. Mateo was surprised yet again. *Meow* sounded the same in Egyptian!

Minister Cox turned the ruby in his ancient fingers. "Oh no!" he said. "I hope Bastet hasn't caused you any trouble. She always likes to fetch me presents."

"Bastet is your pet?" asked Mateo.

The mummy nodded. "I'm very fond of her. My people believe that cats are sacred." He looked sternly at the animal on his lap. "But they can also be rather naughty."

Minister Cox placed the gemstone onto Mateo's palm. Bastet *meowed* sadly as the treasure was taken away. "Stealing is bad behavior," said the mummy. "Look at the trouble you've caused, Bastet."

Mateo yawned and put the ruby into his pocket. "That's okay," he said. "I'm just happy I've solved the mystery. I can barely keep my eyes open!"

Waving goodbye to the mummy, Mateo walked through the dark museum. He was *so* exhausted now, it felt just like a Monday morning. Mateo decided he'd go to bed much earlier from now on. Nothing sounded better than a nice, long sleep.

#1

In halls of bones and gems at night,
A sleepy guard jumps at a sight.
A bandaged friend, a ruby's gleam—
Where am I walking in a dream?

#2

Which word doesn't belong with the others?

Cartouche – Sarcophagus
Obelisk – Stalactite

1. The Carmen Lúcia Ruby is famous for its deep blue color.
2. Some animals, like cats, were mummified in ancient Egypt.
3. A sarcophagus is a stone coffin that can hold an inner wooden coffin.

#3

Which number is the twist (the false one)?

CHAPTER 19

The Migrating Mastodon

SHIVERING, YUKI WADED through the snow. She plowed forward with her eyes shut and both hands in front of her face. As a bitter blizzard blasted her, cold wind screamed into her ears.

"What am I *doing* here?" Yuki wailed. "Why did I run away from home?"

Braving the snowstorm, Yuki opened her eyes. As far as she could see, the world was white. Looking for cover, she ducked behind a nearby boulder. Apart from the large, jagged stones, there wasn't much shelter on the icy plain. Small shrubs shuddered on the ground, trying to shake off their frosty blankets. Watching them tremble, Yuki shivered again. Even the plants wanted to leave this freezing place!

Just then, Yuki remembered why she'd left home. Yesterday evening, her parents surprised her with some *awful* news. "We're moving to New York City!" her dad announced at dinnertime.

"Isn't that great?" her mom asked. "You can play in Central Park!"

Yuki *didn't* think the news was great. Thanks to Mom's job, she'd changed states several times before. She didn't want to move schools *again* and leave her friends behind. Worst of all, she'd have to say goodbye to Jasmine. What if she didn't meet anyone else who watched anime?

As Yuki's tears froze on her cheeks, she stepped back into the blizzard. Closing her eyes, she continued to wade away from home. Suddenly, her hands touched something soft and fluffy.

"I must be asleep," she said with relief. "I'm still in bed and cuddling a plushie."

But Yuki's plushies didn't usually *snort*. Nor did their hot breath swirl around her head. When Yuki looked up, she fell backward into the snow. Somehow, she'd stumbled into a huge and hairy elephant!

"You're m-massive . . ." Yuki stammered. "In fact, you're *mammoth*!"

"I'm not *quite* as big as that," the creature replied. "I'm a mastodon, which is shorter than a mammoth.

My taller cousins have curvier tusks, while mine are shorter and straighter. Mammoths are also heavier mammals, but *don't* say that to their faces."

Yuki stared at the mastodon's tusks. Even if they were shorter, they were still pretty scary! But the ten-foot creature had a kind voice, and his floppy trunk was kind of cute. As he sheltered Yuki from the storm, she started to relax.

"My name's Warren," the mastodon said, "and I'm a vegetarian."

"My name's Yuki," she replied. "Dad and I only eat meat when Mom's not home."

"I'm pleased you live with your parents," Warren replied with a sigh. "I'm hoping to see my family soon."

Yuki frowned. The friendly mastodon had a familiar name. Where had she heard the word *Warren* before? At that moment, a famous fossil flashed before her eyes. She remembered seeing a mastodon skeleton at the Museum of Natural History. Standing tall in the Deep Time exhibition, he'd been unearthed by a man named John C. Warren, but that creature had walked the earth eleven *thousand* years ago.

"If you're alive," Yuki said, "then *this* is the end of the Ice Age."

"You're right!" Warren declared, trumpeting with his trunk. "I can't *wait* till it's over." He tramped away, leaving deep footprints in the snow. "Join me on my journey if you like. I'm heading north."

Yuki stumbled after Warren, following in his huge footsteps. She wondered how the mastodon knew which way was north. There weren't any street signs . . . and there certainly wasn't any sun! As she chased his tail, a worried feeling grew in Yuki's mind. There was something else about Warren's tale she couldn't quite remember.

"Why are you going north?" she shouted above the blizzard.

"To meet my family," he replied. "The land up north is thawing out, which means there are fresh grazing grounds to be found. My mother and sisters have gone ahead to discover new pastures."

"Why are you traveling alone?" Yuki asked. "Did you fight with your family?"

Warren shook his hairy head, showering her with snow. "No," he replied, "most male mastodons travel alone, but I must say, I've been very lonely." He peered down his trunk at her. "How about you? Why are *you* traveling on your own?"

Yuki blushed despite the cold. Suddenly, she felt foolish about running away from home. Warren was eager to find his family, while she was heading in the *other* direction. Looking around at the frozen landscape, she decided to dodge his question.

"It *can't* be the end of the Ice Age," she said. "No *way* is this world getting warmer."

Craaaaaack!

The ground broke beneath Yuki's feet, plunging her into a freezing lake. The cold was so shocking, she couldn't even scream. Luckily, Warren came to Yuki's rescue. With his long trunk, he lifted her to safety.

"Thank y-you." Yuki shuddered, huddling against his warm hide.

"You're welcome," Warren replied. "It seems you were walking on thin ice."

It also seemed that the sudden shock had fixed Yuki's memory. Her trip to the museum was now crystal clear. She remembered that the mastodon's bones had been discovered in a bog. They were found in a town called Newburgh . . . *north* of New York City. As Warren continued on his way, Yuki felt torn in two. She didn't want to tell her friend about his fate, but since he'd saved her life, she *had* to repay the favor.

"Stop!" she pleaded. "You *must* go south. If you don't, you're heading for disaster."

Warren stopped in his tracks. Smiling at Yuki, he shook his head. "We *all* have uncertain futures," he said, "but that can't stop us from moving forward."

Frosty tears fell from Yuki's eyes. "But something bad will happen!" she cried.

"You might *think* it will," the mastodon replied, "but the future is never set in stone. Even when we fear the worst, things don't always turn out as expected."

Warren wandered deeper into the snowstorm. Turning around, he wiggled his ears to wave goodbye to Yuki. "I wish you luck, little girl," he said, "and I hope you find your way home."

The mastodon vanished into the whiteness. A moment later, time seemed to speed up. As the sun and moon raced across the sky, the ice melted in the blink of an eye. The jagged boulders sank to the ground, landing on the grass beside a large lake. Surrounded by the rocks, Yuki smiled with joy. She was standing in the middle of Central Park!

Yuki sat and leaned against a boulder. Warmed by the sunshine, she sighed and closed her eyes. She felt a lot more hopeful now, as if a distant storm had cleared. Maybe her move north to New York wouldn't be as bad as she feared.

#1

I'm furry and huge, with tusks not small.
I walked the Earth when ice covered all.
Not mammoth, but close—I looked
much the same.
Can you guess my Ice Age name?

#2

Which word doesn't belong with the others?

Mastodon – Mammoth
Woolly Rhino – Bison

1. Mastodons and mammoths were both ancient relatives of elephants.
2. Most mastodon fossils have been discovered in North America, often in bogs or swamps.
3. Mastodons survived until the time of the American Revolution in the 1700s.

#3

Which number is the twist (the false one)?

CHAPTER 20

The Wandering Monument

Staring in awe at the massive statue, Kennedy felt tiny. Usually, she didn't mind being little, since Mom said she had a large brain, but as she looked up at the marble man, Kennedy didn't feel big or clever. She realized that she didn't know a great deal about George Washington.

The grand statue had the top spot in the National Museum of American History. He sat on a throne in a flowing robe, like some kind of Roman hero. Kennedy wondered if giant George was tired of raising his hand. Wasn't he bored of the heavy sword he was holding?

Then, the statue moved. He lowered his arm, rolled his shoulders, and wiggled all his toes. "You're right," said George Washington, in a huge, booming voice. "I *would* like to take a break."

As the statue rose to his size-thirty feet, Kennedy stepped backward. It looked like the marble monument wanted to stretch his legs! Luckily, the museum was quiet. As the statue walked toward the exit, nobody tried to stop him. Kennedy struggled to keep up and answer his questions at the same time.

"Do you know who I am?" asked the statue.

Kennedy nodded. "George Washington," she replied.

The statue stopped and glared at her. "You mean *President* Washington."

Kennedy's face went hot. "I know that," she said. "You were the very first President of the United States."

President Washington walked through the exit and onto the plaza outside. The people eating fast-food lunches dropped them and stared.

"What else do you know?" asked the statue. "I'm sure you studied me at school."

"I think you wore a wig in real life," said Kennedy, "and I'm *certain* you had wooden teeth."

The statue's laugh rattled Kennedy's bones. "Wooden teeth? What a terrible idea. Imagine all the splinters!"

Kennedy blushed again. "What about the wig?"

The President shook his head. "That isn't true either." A cool wind blew across the plaza, making the statue shiver. "It's a little chilly out here. I need some warmer clothes."

Crossing the road, President Washington strode across the grass. The marble man was plainly on a mission. Each of his steps was ten of Kennedy's!

"Do you remember the Battle of Yorktown?" he asked.

"No," she replied. "I'm only eight."

The President laughed his booming laugh again. "It was one of the last battles in the American Revolutionary War. In 1781, I was a general. With my French allies, I fought to free this country from British rule. Yorktown was an important port where the enemy forces were hiding, but sadly for Cornwallis, the British commander, I had the town surrounded."

"What happened next?" asked Kennedy, as the President crossed another road.

"After several days of fighting, the general surrendered," the statue replied proudly. "Because of my victory, the British agreed to leave. By 1783, the United States were finally independent."

By now, Kennedy was breathless. It felt like the President was leading her own parade! He rushed inside a red brick building with pretty windows and pointed turrets.

"Where are we?" asked Kennedy, trailing behind. "This isn't a clothes store."

Kennedy was right. This was the Arts and Industries Building, another of the Smithsonian's museums. But when she caught up to the fast-paced President, he *had* found some clothes.

Kennedy peered into the glass case. There was a long--tailed jacket on display, decorated with golden buttons. There were some knee-high trousers, plus a pair of leather boots. They didn't look anywhere near size thirty.

The President sighed sadly. "This used to be my uniform," he said, "but there's no way those clothes will fit me anymore."

As the statue wept a huge marble tear, Kennedy tried to cheer him up. "I'm sorry," she said. "Maybe there's a Big and Tall store nearby."

"I never wore these Roman robes in real life," huffed the President. "But when famous people are turned into monuments, the sculptors sometimes copy ancient costumes."

"That's it!" said Kennedy. "I *know* how to cheer you up. Would you like to see the Washington Monument?"

The President looked excited. When Kennedy pointed him in the right direction, he raced out of the building. As he marched along Independence Avenue, he stopped the traffic. Tires *screeched* and horns *honked* as drivers braked in amazement. Meanwhile, Kennedy broke into a run. Chasing the President, she set a new record for third-grade sprinters!

The Washington Monument was a pointed column, rising high on the National Mall. The granite obelisk could be seen from all over the city. When the President arrived at the memorial, he stood there, stone-still. Standing at the foot of the towering column, the marble man looked tiny.

"Do you... like it?" asked Kennedy, in between breaths. "It was built in your honor."

The President turned around. To her surprise, he was crying again! But Kennedy knew that these were tears of joy.

"It's beautiful," answered the President, "if a little newfangled."

Kennedy giggled. "It's not *new*," she replied. "It's over a hundred years old!"

The statue smiled. "That's something I didn't know."

President Washington and Kennedy sat together on the grass. A crowd of people gathered around them, snapping pictures on their cell phones, but the marble man didn't need much rest. He jumped to his feet and pointed into the distance.

"That must be the White House!" he said. "I never got to live there."

As he marched off again, Kennedy stayed behind. "I'm exhausted!" she explained.

Waving the goodbye, Kennedy thought about everything she'd learned from George Washington. History could be very tiring, but it wasn't boring at all! Behind every statue was an awesome story, just waiting to spring into life. The next time she visited a museum, Kennedy would be ready to run!

But first, she needed a long nap. Lying down on the grass, Kennedy closed her eyes.

#1

I led a fight, both brave and true,
The first President—yes, that's who!
No wooden teeth, though people say.
I helped a nation find its way.
Who am I?

#2

Which word doesn't belong with the others?

Yorktown – Independence
Cornwallis – Mount Vernon

1. George Washington commanded the Continental Army during the American Revolutionary War.
2. George Washington lived in the White House during his presidency.
3. The Washington Monument was completed many years after George Washington's death.

#3

Which number is the twist (the false one)?

Epilogue

The yellow bus rolled back into the schoolyard just as the sun was setting. Inside, sleepy children began to stir, rubbing their eyes and stretching after their long ride.

"Wait till you hear my dream!" one called.

"I flew through space!"

"I met a dinosaur!"

"I chased a steam train!"

"I found buried treasure!"

The bus filled with laughter as the children swapped their stories, each one more fantastic than the last. Their teacher smiled and raised a hand. "Alright, that's enough for today. Tomorrow, you can share them all properly."

At the front of the bus, the strict principal was slumped in his seat, fast asleep. His snores rumbled louder than the engine itself. The children grinned at one another. For once, the noisiest one on the bus wasn't them.

Each book that we have published has **a free audio version available.** To download the audiobook for *Amazing Stories for Curious Minds*, **all you have to do is scan the QR code** or visit: www.littlebigpage.com/cm

If you have any problems or questions, feel free to contact us at help@littlebigpage.com

Answers

CHAPTER 1:
1. A spacecraft (Friendship 7)
2. Submarine
3. 3

CHAPTER 2:
1. The Wright Flyer
2. Parachute
3. 3

CHAPTER 3:
1. Giant squid
2. Seahorse
3. 1

CHAPTER 4:
1. Fire
2. Ice
3. 3

CHAPTER 5:
1. Model T Ford
2. Fuel injector
3. 2

CHAPTER 6:
1. Mummy
2. Telescope
3. 2

CHAPTER 7:
1. Money
2. Credit card
3. 3

CHAPTER 8:
1. Vincent van Gogh
2. Violin
3. 2

CHAPTER 9:
1. Steamboat
2. Stagecoach
3. 1

CHAPTER 10:
1. Dinosaur
2. Stegosaurus
3. 2

CHAPTER 11:
1. Amelia Earhart
2. Jet engine
3. 3

CHAPTER 12:
1. A crystal (tourmaline/elbaite)
2. Marble
3. 1

CHAPTER 13:
1. Pirate
2. Eyepatch
3. 2

CHAPTER 14:
1. Train (steam locomotive)
2. Stetson
3. 3

CHAPTER 15:
1. Hot air balloon
2. Propeller
3. 1

CHAPTER 16:
1. Megalodon
2. Mosasaur
3. 3

CHAPTER 17:
1. Trolley
2. Airplane
3. 2

CHAPTER 18:
1. The museum
2. Stalactite
3. 1

CHAPTER 19:
1. Mastodon
2. Bison
3. 3

CHAPTER 20:
1. George Washington
2. Mount Vernon
3. 2

A NEW ADVENTURE ON EVERY PAGE!

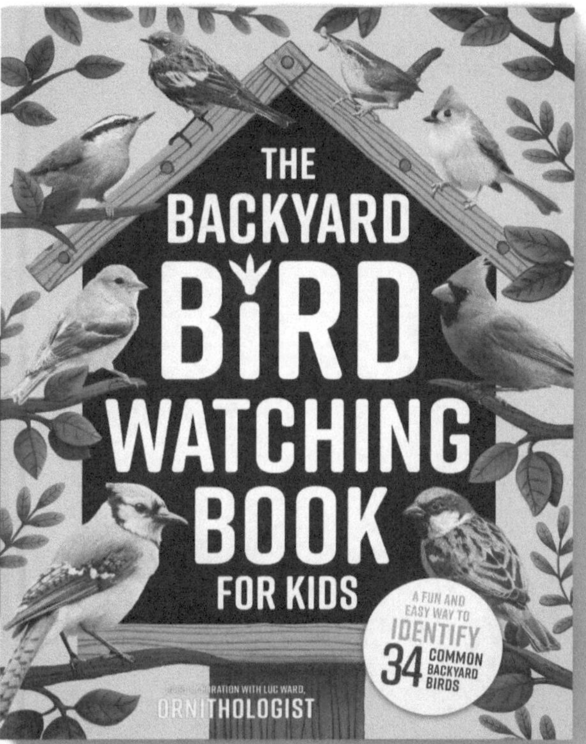

available at amazon

Made in United States
Troutdale, OR
11/20/2025